THE EASTER BOOK

THE EASTER BOOK

CELEBRATION RECIPES, GIFTS AND DECORATIONS

TESSA EVELEGH

▼

PHOTOGRAPHY BY DEBBIE PATTERSON

▼

RECIPES BY JANE SUTHERING

▼

Conran Octopus

For Richard, Zoë, Faye and Dragana

ART DIRECTOR MARY EVANS
DESIGNER PRUE BUCKNALL
PROJECT EDITOR JO MEAD
COPY EDITOR JACKIE MATTHEWS
PRODUCTION JILL MACEY
ILLUSTRATIONS KATE SIMUNEK
CHARTS KING & KING

First published in 1994 by Conran Octopus Limited, 37 Shelton Street, London WC2H 9HN

A CIP record for this book is available from the British Library.

ISBN 1 85029 554 9

Typesetting by op den Brouw Design and Illustration Consultancy, Reading
Printed in Hong Kong

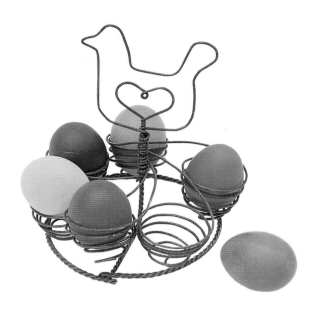

CONTENTS

INTRODUCTION

Nature is at her most exuberant in springtime. Lush foliage, in the freshest lettuce greens, and copious, brilliantly coloured blooms push through seemingly barren earth in an astonishing show of colour. This abundant display, all the more glorious for following the cold, bleak months of winter, has prompted civilizations down the ages to mark the season with a festival.

Our own celebration, Easter, is so entwined in the mists of antiquity, that even its name comes from an ancient pagan festival, celebrated in honour of Eastre, the Anglo-Saxon goddess of spring and fertility. To a large extent, many of today's customs have been absorbed directly from pagan rites. The gift-bearing Easter bunny, for example, is the modern representation of the Easter hare, which was considered to be an incarnation of Eastre. And the egg, now symbolic to Christians of Christ rising from the grave, is an ancient and universal representation of creation and new life.

Easter is the most important festival in the Christian religious calendar, commemorating the death and resurrection of Christ. A moveable feast, its timing is worked out each year according to the first full moon after 21 March which means it can fall any time between 22 March and 25 April; the Eastern Orthodox Church has a slightly different calendar in which the holiday can fall a little later.

It is no accident that Easter coincides with the Jewish Passover, for it was during this feast that Jesus shared his last supper with his disciples. This link is echoed in the names given to Easter by many countries (France, *Pâques*; Italy, *Pasqua*), which derive from *Pesach*, the Hebrew for Passover.

In Christian countries, many customs and traditions centred around eggs have developed over the centuries. As well as dyeing, decorating and eating them, villagers throughout Europe would gather on the green for egg tossing and rolling, commemorating the rolling away of the stone from Christ's tomb. This custom was revived in America, over 150 years ago, by President James Madison's wife who instigated Easter Monday egg rolling on the lawns of Capitol Hill, Washington DC, followed by an Easter Egg Hunt, events which still thrive today.

Lambs are another Easter icon, symbolizing the Paschal Lamb, which was the sacrifice offered at the Passover feast. Later, Christians came to see Jesus himself as the Paschal Lamb, offered as the ultimate sacrifice. Following the Lenten fast, Easter has become a time of great feasting when tender new vegetables are served with celebratory roasted meats. Different countries have developed their own traditional egg dishes, breads and cakes which are specially prepared for the Easter festivities. Chocolate Easter eggs, rabbits and chicks did not appear until the middle of the nineteenth century and, since then, they have become the most popular Easter gifts, exchanged by all generations.

Traditionally, there was a widespread belief that the sun dances for joy on Easter morning, and people used to set off to the hills at sunrise to see the dawn. Certainly, Easter morning, whenever it falls, is the mark that spring has truly arrived. It offers the opportunity to celebrate this, the freshest and most colourful of seasons. The sheer abundance of blossoms, blooms and greenery means there is plenty for the picking with which to deck the home or to offer as gifts.

This book is a celebration of spring, drawing inspiration from Easter customs down the centuries to bring together a joyful collection of things to make, eat and give. Together, they offer all the ingredients for a perfect Easter weekend, yet most can be treasured and enjoyed throughout spring and summer, as well as for years to come.

E A S T E R
TREATS

At Easter, nobody can resist the sensuously rich delights of chocolate. Moulded into eggs, bunnies and chicks, it is the traditional gift, exchanged by all generations. From decorated shortbread to delightful marzipan animals, handmade sweets are always the most appreciated.

CHOCOLATE

Chocolate is a difficult and complicated ingredient to work with at home, and the only way that it becomes easier to handle is with practice. Professional chocolatiers spend years learning the intricacies of chocolate, so do not expect to make something perfectly the first time you try. If you are not happy with your results, do not throw out the chocolate. Gently melt it and use in any recipe calling for melted chocolate, such as sweets, cakes or syrups.

Chocolate is made up of various ingredients, and the most important when you are melting and using chocolate are the cocoa butter – a complex mixture of fats each having a different melting point – and the sugar. If they are not melted correctly, the finished chocolate will not have a shiny finish.

MELTING CHOCOLATE

Chocolate should never come into contact with water or steam when it is melted, as either will cause the chocolate to thicken and lose its shine. There are various methods for melting chocolate, but the easiest one is to melt the chocolate in the oven on its lowest setting. Pre-heat the oven then break the chocolate in

LEFT HANDMADE CHOCOLATE EGGS MAKE THE MOST SPECIAL EASTER GIFTS OF ALL.

even-sized pieces into a clean, dry, heatproof bowl and place it in the oven. The chocolate will melt slowly with no danger of it cooking or burning. Stir the chocolate occasionally until it is smooth.

Chocolate can also be melted over simmering water. Cut or break the chocolate in even-sized pieces, put it in a clean, dry, heatproof bowl and set the bowl over a saucepan of simmering water. Stir until the chocolate is smooth. It is a good idea to wrap a circle of kitchen foil around the top of the pan and set the bowl on the foil. This stops any steam escaping at the side of the pan.

TEMPERING CHOCOLATE

Before you can use chocolate for moulding it must first be warmed and cooled and then warmed again so the fats melt correctly. This technique is known as tempering. Unless chocolate is tempered correctly, it will not set quickly, making it difficult to remove chocolate shapes from their moulds. A sugar thermometer is useful but you can learn to temper chocolate from its appearance. When correctly tempered, it will be liquified but still slightly thick in consistency, and a small blob dropped on a cold surface, such as marble, should set within one minute. Tempered chocolate must be used immediately. If it is left to set and melted again, it must be re-tempered before it can be used for moulding.

To temper chocolate, melt it until smooth then place the bowl of chocolate in a larger one containing cold water and a few ice cubes. Stir the chocolate continuously until some of it sets on the sides and bottom of the bowl. This will happen when the mixture is about 28C/82F.

Warm the bowl of chocolate again until it is just melted and smooth. The temperature of the chocolate at this stage should be cool, about 29C/84F for milk chocolate, 30-31C/86-88F for plain chocolate and 29C/84F for white chocolate.

MOULDING CHOCOLATE

The temperature at which chocolate is moulded is crucial. If it is too hot, a fat bloom (irregular streaks) will appear on the surface as it cools. If it is too cold, a sugar bloom will appear. Blooms on chocolate only detract from the appearance, however, and are not harmful to eat.

HOLLOW EGGS

Moulds are now usually made from Plexiglas, which makes them much easier to deal with than the older-style metal moulds. Whichever type you use, however, the same rules apply. Make sure the mould is completely clean and dry. Polish the inside of the mould with clean cotton wool to ensure the surface is shiny.

There are two ways of actually applying the chocolate. The first method requires a lot of melted chocolate. Using a large pastry brush, coat the inside of each half of the mould with tempered chocolate and leave it in a cool place to set, which can take up to 30 minutes. Then make a second layer by filling each half of the mould completely with melted chocolate, tapping the mould on the surface to remove any air bubbles. Pour out the excess chocolate, leaving the mould evenly coated. Leave to cool until the chocolate is 'waxy' in consistency, then trim the edges with a small sharp knife to leave a smooth rim.

The alternative method requires far less chocolate. Pour enough tempered chocolate into each half of the mould to come about one-third of the way up the sides, then carefully swirl the chocolate around to coat the mould in an even layer. For both methods, leave the chocolate to set until it is completely brittle. It is better to leave the moulds to set in a cool draught, than in the refrigerator where condensation can affect the chocolate.

To remove the moulds, gently tap them on a hard surface and the chocolate should pop out. If the chocolate does not loosen, gently tap the mould a few more times. If you still have difficulty, place the mould in the freezer for about 5 minutes. Resist the temptation to loosen the chocolate with the tip of a knife, as you could easily damage the edge.

Once the moulds have been removed, join the two chocolate halves together. Warm the edges very slightly by sitting the chocolate shapes on a warmed baking tray for a second or two, or by running a hot palette knife over the surface. (Heat the knife over a flame and not in hot water.) As soon as both surfaces are slightly melted, press them together and hold them for a few moments until they are set in position. Balance the egg in a ramekin or a bowl and leave until completely set, which can take up to 30 minutes.

SMALL SOLID EGGS

Polish the mould halves with clean cotton wool, then fill them with tempered chocolate. Leave to harden, then press the shapes out of the moulds with your fingers. To join two halves, place them on a warm baking tray flat-side down for a second or two until level, then press together. Leave in a cool, dry place to set completely.

Harlequin eggs can be made by sticking differently coloured halves together, such as dark chocolate and white chocolate.

CHOCOLATE RUNOUTS

Choose a template, such as an egg shape, rabbit or chick (see pages 122-3) and draw the outline in pencil on a sheet of baking parchment. Stick the baking parchment to a tray with a few dots of melted chocolate, then, using a greaseproof paper piping bag fitted with a fine writing nozzle, follow the outline of your shape. Leave to set.

Spoon melted chocolate into the centre and, using a small skewer or cocktail stick, work it towards the edges to fill the shape completely. Tap the tray on the work surface to remove air bubbles, then leave in a cool dry place to set.

The Easter eggs for the Chocolate Gateau on pages 116-17 are about 5cm/2in high and are made with white chocolate, piped with a tiny bow of melted milk chocolate.

PIPING WITH CHOCOLATE

Adding a few drops of sugar syrup to melted and cooled chocolate will make it easier to pipe. The amount you add will depend on the type of chocolate, but as a rough guide use 15 drops to every 115g/4oz milk or plain chocolate and about 25 drops to 115g/4oz white chocolate.

Use the sugar syrup made for the Chocolate Gateau on pages 116-17, but omit the liqueur. Adding the syrup is a matter of practice, so always add it drop by drop and stir well. If the chocolate hardens, warm it gently again and leave to cool to a piping consistency.

CHOCOLATE PASTE RIBBONS

Add light corn syrup to melted chocolate and leave to cool, to produce a malleable paste which can

be rolled out, cut into ribbons and shaped into decorative bows. The paste will set hard and brittle.

115g/4oz plain chocolate, broken into even pieces
4 tbsp light corn syrup or golden syrup
or
115g/4oz white chocolate, broken into even pieces
2 tbsp light corn syrup or golden syrup

Place the chocolate in a heatproof bowl with the syrup. Warm gently over simmering water, stirring, until just melted. Remove from the heat, stir and leave to cool. Alternatively, you can heat the mixture in the microwave on a medium-high setting (70%) until just melted, checking and

ABOVE MOULDED EASTER EGGS DECORATED WITH CHOCOLATE PASTE RIBBONS AND PIPED WITH MELTED CHOCOLATE.

stirring at 30 second intervals. Turn out on to a marble slab and knead until smooth and cool.

Either use the paste straight away or wrap in cling film and a polythene bag or store in a polythene container in a cool place.

To use, knead the paste until it becomes malleable once more – the heat of your hand should be sufficient. Roll out on a marble slab lightly sprinkled with icing sugar, if necessary, to prevent the paste from sticking. Cut out ribbons, shape bows and attach to the chocolate eggs by pressing and leave to set firm.

MARZIPAN ANIMALS

Marzipan was a traditional Easter sweetmeat long before chocolate grew in popularity. These marzipan Easter animals are decorated with Royal Icing (see page 17) and with edible food colouring. For the eyes you will need tiny dots of piped melted chocolate which have been left to harden. Before beginning, read through the instructions and assemble the necessary equipment. For decorating you will need greaseproof paper piping bags fitted with fine writing nozzles, a small knife and a fine paint brush.

The shapes can take at least 24 hours to firm and harden. This is important because they can develop mould if not left to dry out

ABOVE IRRESISTIBLE MARZIPAN RABBITS AND CHICKS ACCOMPANIED BY VIBRANT LADYBIRDS AND PASTEL EGGS ROLLED IN COLOURED SUGAR. THE SHAPED BISCUITS ARE MADE FROM THE LEMON SHORTBREAD ON PAGE 17 AND FROM TRADITIONAL GINGERBREAD (RECIPE NOT INCLUDED).

completely. Store the shapes in airtight containers. Animals or eggs made with Marzipan will keep for two to three weeks.

MARZIPAN

This marzipan is made without raw egg. If you do not have a sugar thermometer, the sugar syrup is at the soft ball stage when it forms a small, soft ball if it is dropped into a bowl of very cold water.

Makes a generous 450g/1lb

225g/8oz caster sugar
pinch of cream of tartar
225g/8oz ground almonds
½ tsp lemon juice
1 tsp orange flower water, or a few
drops natural almond essence

Put the sugar, cream of tartar and 125ml/4fl oz water in a small saucepan over low heat and stir until the sugar and cream of tartar are dissolved. Bring to the boil and boil until the temperature on a sugar thermometer reads 116C/240F or is at the soft ball stage.

Immediately remove the syrup from the heat and stir in the ground almonds, lemon juice and orange flower water, if using, with a wooden spoon. Mix to a firm paste. Flavour with a few drops of almond essence at this stage, if using instead of the flower water.

As soon as the mixture is cool enough to handle, transfer it to a marble slab or plastic board and knead until smooth and cool. Wrap in cling film and keep in the refrigerator. This paste will keep for two to three weeks.

RABBIT

To make a rabbit, you need 45g/1½oz uncoloured marzipan and two tiny balls of pink-coloured marzipan – one slightly larger than the other. These make the nose and tail .

Divide the uncoloured marzipan into two pieces – one twice the size of the other. Shape each piece into an elongated pear-shape, then make a cut in the pointed end of each piece. The larger piece will be the body.

Position the larger piece of marzipan with the cut facing towards you. Twist each cut piece outwards in a quarter turn to make the legs.

The smaller piece of marzipan is used for the head. Holding it in your hand, with the cut at the top, twist the two cut pieces backwards in a quarter turn to make the ears.

Press the head on to the body, then stick on the nose and tail, with a tiny blob of royal icing.

Using a greaseproof paper piping bag fitted with a fine writing nozzle, pipe two eyes with royal icing, then top each with a tiny chocolate dot.

Using a fine paint brush dipped in black edible colouring, make three dots on either side of the nose and three lines on each foot. Leave the rabbit in a cool, dry place to harden.

CHICK

To make a chick, you need 55g/2oz yellow-coloured marzipan and a tiny amount of orange-coloured marzipan for the beak.

For the top of the chick's head, roll out a tiny amount of yellow marzipan, then twist it into a coil.

Divide the remaining yellow marzipan to give a generous third and a mean two-thirds. Shape both pieces into balls – the small one is for the head. Shape the larger ball so it has a pointed end, which will represent the tail feathers. Make a cut in either side of the body to form the wings, then score a few lines along each wing for feathers with a small knife. Score markings around the tail as well.

Set the head on to the body, then set the coil of marzipan on the head. Make two indentations on either side of the head with the handle of a small spoon to form the eye sockets. Using a greaseproof paper piping bag fitted with a fine writing nozzle, pipe two eyes with royal icing, then top each with a tiny chocolate drop. Shape the orange marzipan for the beak and press it into position. Leave the chick in a cool, dry place to harden.

BELOW THE RABBIT AND CHICK ARE CONSTRUCTED FROM SIMPLE SHAPES.

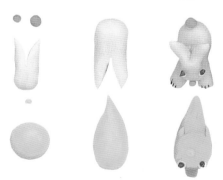

EASTER BASKET BISCUITS

Makes 12-14

LEMON SHORTBREAD
200g/7oz plain flour
30g/1oz rice flour
150g/5oz butter, softened, plus extra
for greasing trays
85g/3oz icing sugar, sifted
finely grated rind of ½ lemon

MALLOW PASTE
2 tsp powdered gelatine
2 tsp white fat
400g/14oz icing sugar, plus extra for
rolling
green and yellow edible food colourings

TO ASSEMBLE THE BASKETS
1 egg white, lightly beaten
about 4 tbsp Royal Icing

Lightly grease two baking trays with butter and pre-heat the oven to 160C/325F/Gas 3.

Sift the flour and rice flour together, then rub in the butter until the mixture resembles fine crumbs. Stir in the sugar and lemon rind and knead to form a firm, pliable dough.

Roll out the dough on a lightly floured surface until about 3mm/⅛in thick and cut out basket shapes using the template on page 124. With a small knife, mark weave lines on the shapes. Place on the baking trays and bake for about 15 minutes until lightly golden. Cool on a wire rack.

To decorate, make six primroses and four leaves for each basket using mallow paste coloured with food colouring. Once hard, attach these to the basket with royal icing.

To make the mallow paste, place the gelatine, fat and 3 tbsp water in a small heatproof bowl set over a saucepan of simmering water and heat gently until dissolved, stirring.

Sift the icing sugar into a bowl, then stir in the warm liquid. Turn out on to a surface lightly dusted with icing sugar and knead until smooth and cold. Wrap in cling film and then a tightly sealed polythene bag and store in the refrigerator.

To shape the primroses, use pale yellow paste. Roll out the paste thinly on a surface lightly sprinkled with icing sugar. Stamp out five tiny heart shapes for each flower (an aspic cutter is useful for this). Press the five points together, sticking them with egg white. Leave on a sheet of baking parchment until set and hardened, up to 24 hours. Paint fine lines in the centre of each flower with edible yellow food colouring.

To shape the leaves, use green paste. Roll out the paste thinly. Stamp out appropriate leaf shapes with small cutters or use a template. Mark veins on the leaves with a small sharp knife, then leave to harden.

ROYAL ICING
Makes about 225g/8oz

1 egg white
225g/8oz icing sugar, sifted
1 tsp lemon juice

Lightly whisk the egg white in a bowl. Beat in the icing sugar, 1 spoonful at a time. When half the icing sugar has been added, beat in the lemon juice, then continue adding the icing sugar until a firm texture is reached. The icing can be stored in the refrigerator for up to a week.

LEFT AND ABOVE LEMON SHORTBREAD BASKETS MAKE DELICIOUS EASTER GIFTS.

DECORATED
EGGS

Symbolic of new life and fertility since pagan times, eggs have come to represent the resurrection. For centuries, eggs have been embellished and exchanged at Easter, resulting in a rich inheritance of traditional crafts. Ranging from simply dyed shells to intricate works of art, they can add colour to the Easter egg hunt or become precious gifts to treasure.

DYED EGGS

Coloured eggs instantly evoke the image of Easter. Adding them to floral decorations transforms a simple spring arrangement into something festive. Placing them on the breakfast table revives that childhood thrill of anticipating a special day.

Yet, for all the magic they bring, eggs are easy to colour. Being naturally porous, they take the pigment well, and the charm of dyeing them is that each egg holds an element of surprise. The imperfections of their shells and their individual 'skin tones' affect the way the dye takes, resulting in marbled and speckled effects.

In the past, natural dyes were used, but nowadays, there is a far wider palette to choose from: egg-dyeing kits and food colourings for eggs that are to be eaten; or a rainbow of fabric dyes for those that are not. If the eggs are to be eaten, or likely to be subjected to a bit of rough and tumble in the Easter egg hunt, they should be hard boiled first. Put them into a pan of cold water and bring them slowly to the boil to avoid cracking, then simmer for a further ten minutes. Eggs to keep should be dyed raw in a cold solution and blown afterwards; empty shells would float and weighting them down could damage them.

To prepare the dye, mix the pigment – either half a bottle of food colouring or half a disc of fabric dye – into about ½ litre/1 pint of hot water. Add two tablespoons of vinegar and one of salt as fixative. The mixture should be a very deep shade – if it is not, add more pigment. Stir well and allow to cool. Lower the eggs in and leave until the shells have become the desired shade. Drain them on kitchen paper and either leave natural or polish with a little olive oil.

Once the eggs are completely dry, they can be blown. Very carefully make a small hole at each end with a darning needle and, holding the egg over a bowl, blow out the contents. Rinse the shells in warm water and allow them to dry.

LEFT THE CHALKY GOLD OF TURMERIC AND THE BURNISHED COPPER OBTAINED FROM ONION SKINS SIT COMFORTABLY WITH BRIGHTER, MAN-MADE COLOURS.

LEFT FERNS, PRIMROSES, AND EVEN THE LEAVES OF AN INDOOR GRAPE IVY MAKE EXCELLENT PRINTING PLATES.

RIGHT A LEAF OR FLOWER, AN OLD PAIR OF TIGHTS AND SOME DYE ARE ALL THAT IS NEEDED TO TURN EGGS INTO DELICATE WORKS OF ART.

LEAF PRINTS

Through the ages artists have striven to imitate the beauty of nature, and there is no better way than to make a print directly from the original. With practice, even those who are unsure of their artistic abilities can produce exquisite designs using spring flowers and leaves as stencils when dyeing eggs. The prints can be made on undyed eggs to let the natural shell colour show through. Alternatively, they can be applied to eggs that have already been dyed to a pale shade. This allows the flower or leaf motif to appear as a contrasting tone: the dye bleeds delicately around the edges and along leaf veins, sometimes appearing in slightly different hues.

The finer and flatter the original leaf or flower is, the better the end result will be, as these hug the egg closely making a better mask.

Place the leaf or flower on the egg, flattest side down (this is usually the upper side). Lay a square cut from a pair of nylon tights over the egg and tie tightly at the back. The leaves and petals will spread slightly as the nylon is tightened around the egg, so compensate for this in your arrangement. Lower this package into the dye and let the background colour develop. When you are happy with the shade, remove the egg from the dye. Allow the egg to dry out completely before cutting away the nylon.

2 3

NATURAL DYES

For centuries, the delicate, moody tones of natural dyes were the only option for colouring eggs. Some of these shades are still easily created using ingredients from the larder; others require dyes that are not so readily available and which are mainly supplied by mail order specialists (see page 126). Highly effective yet cheap and easy, onion skins produce a range of hues from subtle yellow through to burnished copper; red onion skins give more ruby tones. For a more vivid, chalky yellow use turmeric (see page 20).

More difficult to get hold of but worth the effort for their subtle shades are brazilwood (or redwood, as it is sometimes called), for red tones from dusky pink to deep crimson, and logwood for moody purples and denim blues. Although these are natural products, they are not suitable for dyeing eggs that will be eaten, nor should they be boiled up in saucepans that are used for cooking food.

Whatever dye source you use, the pigment will have to be extracted by boiling. Use either six onion skins, or two tablespoons of turmeric, brazilwood or logwood in about 1½ litres/3 pints of water. Add two tablespoons of vinegar to intensify the colour, then simmer until a deep tone is achieved. Add more pigment at this stage if necessary and continue

simmering until you are satisfied that the shade is deep enough.

If the eggs are going to be eaten, they can be boiled for ten minutes in the dye. If they are already cooked leave them in the cooled solution for up to half an hour. The solution must also be cold for eggs that are to be kept as these will need to be blown afterwards (see page 21) and any heat in the liquid will slightly cook and solidify the contents.

Remove the eggs with a wooden spoon to avoid damaging the delicate film of colour and drain on kitchen paper. When they are completely dry, either leave them with their natural, chalky finish, or polish them with a little olive oil.

The joy of colouring with natural materials is that each dye behaves in a slightly different way. But as you acquire the dyer's skills, and learn about the individual qualities of each dye, the palette broadens. Once you are confident with single-pigment dyes, you can mix the colours. For example, dyeing an egg pale yellow using turmeric, then dipping it in a blue solution of logwood can turn the shell a deep olive green.

ENGRAVED EGGS

Engraved eggs are traditional in continental Europe, where many countries have developed their own distinctive styles. In the Ukraine, Lithuania and Poland, the designs are often geometric, while Switzerland favours flora, fauna and houses. However, they all share a charming simplicity. As eggs are engraved by scratching a design on to dyed shells to reveal the natural shell colour underneath, large areas of complicated engraving could weaken the shells.

Start with a simple design, such as a name and date and progress to something more ambitious once you have gained confidence. An effective way to develop a design is to section the egg, either in concentric rings, or with a longitudinal line dividing it into 'front' and 'back'.

Use a scalpel or craft knife in a scratching action rather than long, clean sweeps which could appear uneven. It is better to move forward only 2cm/¾in at a time, going back over the line, before moving on.

LEFT SIMPLE LINE IMAGES ARE EASY TO REPRODUCE WHILE GIVING THE EGGS AUTHENTIC APPEAL.

RIGHT TRADITIONALLY, EGGS WERE ENGRAVED WITH A SHORT EASTER MESSSAGE.

BATIK EGGS

The brilliantly coloured Pisanki eggs that are made in many East European countries are not difficult to reproduce at home, but they do require patience, practice and care.

Using the batik wax-resist method of dyeing, the patterns are gradually built up, starting with the palest colour and finishing with the darkest, which traditionally was almost black. Fabric dyes, which come in a broad palette of colours, are highly effective for this process (see page 21).

Work directly on to the shell. A pencilled design could smudge and be difficult to follow as successive dyes mask the lines. Keep it simple – even a series of zigzags running round the egg can be effective if done in rich, glowing colours.

WORKING WITH WAX

Begin by dipping the egg halfway into a pale dye, such as yellow, to give a guideline round the middle. Once that has dried, the egg is ready for its first wax pattern.

Draw the design on the egg with hot wax using a *kistkas* – a special tool with a tiny metal funnel mounted on to a wooden stick. Put a small piece of beeswax into the top of the funnel, and heat over a candle until the beeswax runs through the tiny hole in the other end. *Tjanting* tools, or batik needles from the Far East, old pen nibs and pins can also be used as drawing tools, each creating different effects, depending on their thickness.

Dip the egg into the first dye colour. As the wax resists the dye, this first part of the design will show through as natural shell colour on the finished egg once the wax has been melted off. When the egg is dry, draw on the second part of the design in wax and dip the egg in a darker dye. This will appear as the palest coloured part of the finished design.

For more complicated designs, repeat the procedure using increasingly darker dyes; by the time the egg comes out of the final dye, it can look almost black. Carefully melt off the layers of wax over a candle rubbing gently with a cloth as the wax softens to remove any candle soot.

RIGHT INTRICATE DESIGNS CAN BE BUILT UP IN LAYERS OF COLOURED DYES.

1. HEAT THE FUNNEL OF THE KISTKAS UNTIL
THE BEESWAX INSIDE IS FLUID ENOUGH TO
DRAW WITH.

2. DRAW THE FIRST PART OF THE DESIGN IN
WAX. THIS WILL SHOW AS NATURAL SHELL
ON THE FINISHED EGG.

3. DIP THE EGG IN RED DYE FOR A FEW
MINUTES TO COLOUR IT PINK – A STRONGER
SHADE WOULD MASK SUCCESSIVE COLOURS.

4. DRAW THE NEXT PART OF THE DESIGN IN
WAX, THEN PUT THE EGG INTO A JAR OF
ORANGE DYE.

5. LEAVE THE EGG IN THE ORANGE DYE
UNTIL IT DEVELOPS A DEEP TONE THAT WILL
CONTRAST WITH THE PINK.

6. DRAW ON THE FINAL PART OF THE DESIGN
AND DYE PURPLE. WHEN THE EGG IS DRY,
MELT OFF THE WAX AND GENTLY POLISH.

1. APPLY GLUE TO THE EGG AND WIND ON THE STRING IN SCROLL FORMATIONS.

2. COAT WITH AN OPAQUE PAINT, ALLOW TO DRY, THEN PAINT WITH TWO COATS OF GOLD SIZE.

3. WHEN THE GOLD SIZE IS ALMOST DRY, APPLY THE DUTCH METAL LEAF. FINISH WITH A COAT OF SHELLAC VARNISH.

4. BY GILDING ONLY OVER THE STRING, THE PAINTED UNDERCOAT WILL CREATE A PATTERN.

GILDED EGGS

In 1290, the English king, Edward I, ordered eggs to be decorated with gold leaf for presentation to favoured members of his court. Today, Dutch metal leaf can be used to give stunning gilded results without the expense and difficulties of working with real gold leaf.

Prepare the eggs by blowing and washing them out (see page 21), then paint the shells with a water based opaque paint such as Plaka. Once this is completely dry, paint with gold size – a special adhesive used with gold leaf. When the gold size is almost dry (see the individual manufacturer's instructions), carefully press the metal leaf on to the egg, and peel away its protective tissue. Allow the egg to dry out for a day, then gently polish with cotton wool to rub away some of the

ABOVE THESE GOLDEN EGGS HAVE BEEN GIVEN A RICH UNDERCOAT OF COLOUR FOR EXTRA DEPTH AND TO GIVE THE APPEAR-ANCE OF ANTIQUE GILDING.

gold and reveal hints of colour underneath. To prevent the metal leaf from tarnishing, finish off with a final coat of shellac varnish.

As an alternative to smooth golden eggs, give them a texture before gilding. Even ordinary household string can be used to great effect.

BEADED EGGS

From humble beginnings, the East European folk art of simply dyed Easter eggs became ever more elaborate and intricate. Eventually, they came to be used as love tokens, the depth of affection measured by the amount of painstaking work applied to so transient a canvas. The Polish custom of banging eggs together to see whose would break first did nothing to diminish the effort put into embellishing boiled eggs destined to be smashed and eaten.

Decorating Easter eggs first became popular on a wide scale in Europe during the thirteenth century. Red, symbolizing Christ's blood, was the traditional colour. In Russia, the shells of these eggs were scattered on the graves of relatives on Easter Sunday. On the same day in Poland, dyed eggs were taken to church to be blessed by the priest, a custom still practised by some.

In many countries, egg decoration became the preserve of single girls who competed to create ever more elaborate and intricate designs that could be presented as love tokens.

The ultimate egg love token was presented by Tsar Alexander III to his wife, the Tsarina Dagma, in 1884. It was the first egg to be commissioned from the royal goldsmith, Peter Carl Fabergé. Made of gold and white enamel, its golden 'yolk' contained a miniature, ruby-eyed gold hen, which in turn opened up to reveal a tiny imperial crown set with diamonds.

Fabergé's style subsequently fired the imaginations of generations of egg decorators to produce elaborately decorated eggs, some carefully hinged and satin-lined, and some, like the original, opening up to reveal a gift. A far cry from those real eggs that were decorated to last but a day, these jewelled versions are treasured, collected, and displayed.

The beauty of eggs elaborately decorated at home lies in the individuality of each one. The romantic, richly beaded, braided and brocaded eggs in Louis XVI style shown here, have been evolved and perfected over the years by their maker. Smoothly wrapping fabric around an egg shape is very difficult to do, but you can create a similarly opulent effect using paint and even découpage as a background for beading.

Goose eggs may be more suitable than hens' for the more elaborate eggs – partly because they provide a much larger area for decoration and partly because they are considerably stronger. However, goose eggs do

RIGHT THE RICH, ALL-ROUND DECORATION OF THESE OPULENT EGGS IS EFFORTLESSLY SHOWN OFF BY HANGING THEM ON STRINGS OF GLASS BEADS IN FRONT OF A MIRROR.

1. PAINT A BLOWN GOOSE EGG WITH AN OPAQUE PAINT SUCH AS POSTER OR SATIN-FINISH HOUSEHOLD PAINT.

2. PASTE ON AN EASTER ARRANGEMENT, CUT FROM A GREETINGS CARD OR OLD PRINT. SEAL THE EGG WITH ARTISTS' VARNISH AND ALLOW IT TO DRY BEFORE APPLYING THE BEADED EDGING.

3. PLACE BROAD BANDS OF BEADS IN PERFECT ROWS BY LEAVING THE STRINGS IN PLACE UNTIL THE GLUE IS FULLY DRY.

sometimes come in extraordinary shapes, and need to be hand-picked at farms or quality grocers.

One of the most basic difficulties egg decorators face is how to hold the egg while painting the whole surface evenly, without smudging or risking paint joins by painting in sections. One answer is to pass a fine skewer or knitting needle through the blow holes. This can then be laid on top of a bowl and the egg carefully rotated as it is painted.

The best adhesive to use for fixing any kind of decoration to an egg is a high-tack crafter's glue. It starts off opaque, so is easy to see while being applied, but dries clear. It also allows enough time before it sets for pieces to be moved around, yet is tacky enough to hold them in position while working.

For straight-line beading, buy the beads that are sold on strings in craft shops, and glue them, still strung, into position. Wait until the adhesive is fully dry before removing the strings. Using this method, it is not difficult to cover an egg completely with tiny beads, the beads looking like stitches in fabric. Try using strings in alternating colours to create stripes, or even restring the beads to make elaborately coloured patterns.

FAR LEFT RICH BEADING PROVIDES TAPESTRY-LIKE INSPIRATION. THIS EFFECT CAN BE ECHOED USING A DÉCOUPAGE IMAGE.

E A S T E R
GIFTS

Giving at Easter still reflects the spirit of yesteryear when the love, effort, and obvious enjoyment of putting presents together mattered so much more than their commercial value. Handmade can mean something as simple as packing an Easter basket for the day, or creating something more long-lasting, like stitching a sampler to commemorate a special year.

EASTER BASKETS

Many traditional Easter gifts – decorated eggs, flowers, chocolate and other candy treats – hold few inherent surprises. But since these presents are so decorative in themselves, they deserve to be shown off rather than covered up. In short, Easter gifts should be not so much wrapped as gloriously presented.

Baskets overflowing with small presents for the whole family make a wonderful gift, evocative of abundant hampers from a bygone age. Buy a brand new wicker basket as part of the present, or revive an old one by painting it in a springtime tone. Spraying on the colour is the most successful method, as using a brush leaves paint clogged in the weave. Car spray paints are readily available and offer a wide choice of colours. To create an antique look with glimpses of the natural willow showing through, simply spray the paint straight on to the untreated willow. It will flake in areas where the surface is at its smoothest. This can be enhanced a little by gentle sanding with a fine glass paper. Line with paper or fabric before filling.

LEFT TRIM BASKETS WITH RIBBONS, BOWS
AND EVEN NESTS, THEN FILL TO BURSTING
WITH EASTER GOODIES.

LEFT FOIL-WRAPPED AND SUGAR EGGS ARE
BEST SHOWN OFF IN GLASS JARS, STACKED
INTO A WIRE MILK CRATE.

The thrill of packed baskets is that they offer glimpses of their contents, while keeping secret the nature of items yet to be unpacked.

This idea can be extended to all kinds of easily portable containers which, if they are particularly relevant to the recipient, can become the present itself. Green-fingered friends, for example, would be delighted with a seed tray packed with gardening delights (plus a chocolate egg or three). And who would not be enchanted by a prettily painted Somerset trug filled with handmade Easter biscuits?

Baskets and other containers lend themselves to witty displays of chocolate animals. The very best-quality chocolate creatures are wrapped in cellophane, rather than foil, to show off the full glossy detail of the chocolatier's craft. You can either pack these in a traditional basket as they are, or remove the cellophane and tuck them into alternative containers. Who could resist chocolate chickens roosting in old-fashioned terracotta pots? And what lady would not be delighted to open an exquisite hat box to find chocolate baby bunnies snuggling in folds of tissue?

LEFT A BIRDCAGE BECOMES AN ELABORATE
BASKET FOR REALISTIC SUGAR EGGS.

SUBSTITUTED FOR A BASKET, A PACKED SEED
TRAY CAN LATER BE PUT TO GOOD USE
BY GARDENERS.

NOT AN EASTER BONNET IN THE HAT BOX –
BUT CHOCOLATE BABY BUNNIES LAUGHING
AT THE JOKE.

STRING HANDLES TURN TERRACOTTA POTS
INTO RUSTIC BASKETS FIT FOR ROOSTING
CHOCOLATE CHICKENS.

EASTER BASKET BISCUITS ARE TOO PRETTY TO
HIDE – A LONG FLAT SOMERSET TRUG MAKES
A PERFECT DISPLAY.

PASTA NESTS

Nests of coloured pasta brimming with brightly dyed hard-boiled eggs make a charmingly simple Easter table decoration. Ribbons of fresh pasta are traditionally sold already twisted into portion-sized nests so all that needs to be added is a trio of eggs. Position the eggs while the pasta is still soft; once dry it will hold the eggs securely in place.

All good Italian delicatessens offer the standard buttermilk-coloured egg noodles, though the variously shaded fresh pastas are a little more difficult to find. Black pasta *(al nero di seppia)* is tinted with cuttlefish ink; the red *(alla bietola)*, with beetroot, and the green *(verde)*, with spinach.

If you cannot buy any of the colourful varieties, you can still achieve a festive look through the eggs. Food colourings offer a range of safe-to-eat shades which can be used to subtle or vivid effect, depending on how long you leave the eggs in the dyes. Here, the bronze eggs have been dyed using onion skins and the yellow ones using turmeric (see page 24). The soft green and the more extrovert, vivid turquoise colour were achieved using food colourings.

RIGHT FRESH PASTA NESTS CONTAINING CLUTCHES OF DYED EGGS.

PAPIER-MÂCHÉ GIFT BOXES

For generations, children in continental Europe have come down to breakfast on Easter morning to be greeted by an array of brightly decorated cardboard eggs, each containing a surprise gift. Following this custom, these charming, egg-shaped papier-mâché boxes are likely to become treasured themselves, long outliving their contents.

Decoration can be as simple as zigzags or spots if you are not a confident painter. For a more sophisticated effect, try using découpage. Paint the papier-mâché egg then stick down images using polyvinyl adhesive. When the design is dry, apply a coat of diluted PVA to varnish and seal the egg.

MOULDING THE GIFT BOXES

MATERIALS
Round balloon(s)
Strips of card
Newspaper
Wallpaper paste
Scalpel
White household emulsion paint
Acrylic paints
PVA adhesive
Polyurethane varnish

Tear the newspaper into strips about 15cm/6in long by 2.5cm/1in wide and blow up the balloon until it is about 15cm/6in in length.

Using plenty of paste, cover the balloon with one layer of overlapping paper strips placed top to bottom then cover it again, this time placing the strips horizontally across the first ones. Repeat the whole process once more and allow to dry for a day. Over the next couple of days repeat this two more times, until you have built up 12 layers of newspaper strips. Allow the egg to dry out.

When the papier mâché is hard and dry, draw a central line lengthwise round the egg. Using a scalpel and following the line, cut right through the papier mâché and the balloon to divide the egg into two equal halves. Remove the scraps of burst balloon.

For the lip cut two strips of card, one 1cm/⅜in wide, the other 2cm/¾in wide to fit snugly inside the cut edge of the egg. Glue the narrow strip inside the rim of on half, aligning the top edge of the cardboard with the top edge of the papier mâché. Trim the strip to fit the egg if necessary. Allow to dry.

Glue the wider strip over the narrow one, aligning their bottom edges so that the top of the wider

RIGHT FANTASY BIRDS ADD TO THE APPEAL OF THESE BRIGHTLY COLOURED EGG-SHAPED GIFT BOXES.

1. PASTE 12 LAYERS OF PAPER STRIPS ON TO A
PARTIALLY BLOWN UP BALLOON, ALTER-
NATING THE DIRECTION OF THE LAYERS.

strip projects above the egg's rim by
1cm/⅜in. Allow to dry out completely. Trim the strip to fit.

Glue one layer of newspaper
strips over the lip, then completely
cover the egg with one more layer of
strips, covering the hole left by the
balloon's knot. Leave to dry out
completely.

Paint the egg all over with white
household emulsion and allow to
dry. Decorate the egg with Easter
birds or patterns using bright acrylic
paints and, when dry, finish with
polyurethane varnish.

LEFT A FISTFUL OF JELLYBEANS BECOMES AN
EXCITING SURPRISE WHEN HIDDEN INSIDE A
PAPIER-MÂCHÉ EGG.

2. WHEN THE EGG HAS DRIED OUT COMPLETELY, DRAW A CENTRAL LINE ROUND THE EGG LENGTHWISE.

3. USING A SCALPEL, CUT ALONG THE LINE TO OPEN THE EGG, BURSTING THE BALLOON AT THE SAME TIME.

4. FORM A LIP TO HOLD THE TWO HALVES TOGETHER BY GLUING CARD STRIPS TO THE RIM OF ONE HALF .

5. SECURE THE LIP WITH MORE PAPER STRIPS. ALLOW TO DRY THEN DECORATE AND VARNISH.

EGG AND FEATHER WREATH

In many cultures, the handsome, newly-moulted show feathers of courting male birds were often collected and woven into wreaths at Easter time. They were traditionally adorned with painted eggs, turning the circle into a symbol for rebirth. With a few easily obtainable materials you can adapt this idea to make a welcoming Easter decoration for your front door.

Many craft shops sell small feathers by the bagful but offer the larger, more showy ones individually which means you can hand-pick them yourself. The superstitious will need to take care, however, as the elaborate feathers of some birds traditionally carry rather sinister connotations. Magpies, for example, were regarded as evil, while peacock feathers were believed to cause infertility if brought indoors. There is, nonetheless, a wide choice of feathers, including those from gamebirds and domesticated fowl. These range from the russet tones of pheasants' tail feathers to the brilliant shades of blue, green and gold provided by

LEFT THE TAIL FEATHERS OF MALE PHEAS-
ANTS FRAME A STRIKING WREATH.

exotic ducks and some bantam roosters.

A feather wreath, unlike many floral decorations, can be packed away to be used again year after year, perhaps given a new appearance with freshly decorated eggs.

CONSTRUCTING THE WREATH

MATERIALS
*Chicken wire, length of
wreath's circumference by
approximately 30cm/12in
Sphagnum moss
Approximately 20 large feathers
Bag of smaller feathers
10 decorated eggs
Glue gun and glue sticks
Florists' wire*

First make the base. Tightly roll the wire round the moss to make a large sausage. Curve this into a circle and bind the ends together with florists' wire. Then attach the feathers. Ideally, each feather should be wired separately to the wreath, though for speed, they can be fixed using a glue gun. Start by arranging the large feathers into a pleasing formation. Fill in the spaces with plenty of smaller feathers radiating at angles from the base wire. Complete the wreath with decorated eggs. Either use painted wooden eggs or decorate your own fresh eggs and blow them before gluing in position with the heated glue gun.

CROSS-STITCH COCKEREL

Cross-stitch samplers have a universal appeal that transcends time and place. There is nothing over-fussy about this form of embroidery which, since the 1830s, has been worked following charts similar to this one.

Traditionally stitched by young girls, they were often used to commemorate events such as births and marriages, incorporating lettering and dates. It is a delightful idea that can be reproduced today for any event. A small sampler takes only a short time to stitch and, complete with a personalized, embroidered message, makes an original Easter card that can be kept and framed.

MATERIALS
32-count evenweave linen fabric,
30cm/12in square
1 skein each of stranded cotton as
shown in key
1.5m/1⅔yd ribbon, to trim

To centre the motif: fold the linen in half lengthways and work a line of

LEFT A PROUD COCKEREL, INSPIRED BY AN 18TH-CENTURY EMBROIDERY, LENDS A TIME-LESS QUALITY TO THIS EASTER SAMPLER.

KEY One square represents two threads

(yell)	DMC 782		
(sage)	Anchor 843	(pink)	Anchor 10
(dk gn)	DMC 924	(red)	DMC 355

running stitches down the fold. Repeat widthways. These lines cross at the centre of the fabric, and correspond with the thick rules on the chart. Work from the centre outwards. Using one strand of thread and counting two threads of linen for every square, follow the chart to stitch crosses in the correct colours.

To form a cross stitch, start by bringing an unknotted thread up from the back of the work, leaving a long tail, which can be secured later by passing the back of the cross stitches over it. Count two threads across and two threads up, pass the needle through to the back of the work and bring it out to the front again exactly two threads below. Bring it across the original stitch to complete the cross. When working, ensure that the top part of the stitch always goes in the same direction.

When the sampler is complete, measure out 11cm/4⅜in from both lines of central running stitches in both directions and pull out a thread. Cut along the line of removed thread. Remove the central tacking markers. Place the sampler upside down on a thin white towel and gently press with a steam iron, spraying stubborn creases. Using tiny stabbing stitches, bind the sampler with ribbon, making loops at the corners.

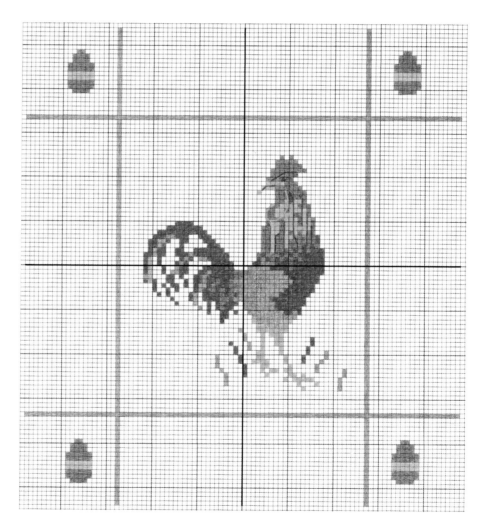

▼▼▼▼▼▼▼▼▼▼▼▼▼▼▼▼

PAPERCUT EASTER CARDS

Papercut collages in soft antique tones make original Easter greetings cards that can later be framed and hung on the wall. Inspired by a combination of traditional Swiss black-and-white papercuts and the more colourful Polish versions, they are built up layer upon layer in differently coloured papers to give depth to the scene.

In their simplest form, papercuts are made by cutting outline shapes with scissors from folded paper which open up into an image of perfect symmetry. The more complex papercuts often incorporate intricate lace effects, or images within frames that have to be cut using a scalpel.

To make a collage papercut card, start by sketching out the whole picture on a sheet of paper and cutting the backing card to size. When you have completed all the papercuts, arrange them on the backing card and glue them into position. They can be glued to the backing card using either a spray adhesive or a paper glue stick. The

LEFT THE PERFECT SYMMETRY OF PAPERCUTS LENDS AN OLD WORLD CHARM TO HANDMADE EASTER GREETINGS.

spray adhesive provides a fine film of glue which stays tacky long enough to allow the pieces to be moved around. The collage can be given more depth by fixing the pieces only where they naturally touch the backing card instead of sticking them down firmly around the edge.

Papercuts can be used for more than cards. The egg wraps shown here are very simple and bring an enchanting seasonal touch to the Easter morning breakfast table. Quick and easy to do, they can be cut mainly using scissors and need only minimal use of a scalpel, or craft knife. They are a perfect introduction

LEFT SOFT DENIM BLUES AND GOLDS ARE SYMPATHETIC COLOURS FOR NATURAL EGGSHELL SHADES.

to papercutting, and can even be used as the ingredients for a collage card. Confident scissor users can then go on to more elaborate scalpel work, such as intricate trellises and lace patterns. Avoid paper that is too thick or very thin. Thick paper will be difficult to cut and thin paper may tear as you work.

CUTTING THE EGG WRAPS

MATERIALS
*A4 sheet of coloured paper
per 4 egg wraps*
Tracing paper
Sharp embroidery scissors
Cutting board
Scalpel
Masking tape
Invisible sticky tape

Trace the designs off this page. Fold the coloured paper in half lengthways. Starting at the top of the sheet, align the fold line on the pattern with the folded edge of the paper. Transfer the design. In the same way, mark out a second design below the first always positioning the fold line on the folded edge of the paper. There should be space for four egg wraps on the sheet of paper.

Use embroidery scissors to cut carefully round the outlines. Using masking tape, fix the still-folded cutout on to a cutting board. Cut round any internal lines, such as the area between the animals' legs, with a scalpel. Unstick and unfold the paper creasing the fold line back to ensure a smooth curve. Fix the papercut round the egg using invisible sticky tape.

PAPIER-MÂCHÉ EGG CUPS

Instead of wrapping up Easter eggs, show them off on the breakfast table in handmade egg cups. This delightful fairytale example, beautifully decorated in delicate shades of turquoise and parchment, is made from papier mâché – newspaper strips and scraps of corrugated card magically recycled into an exquisite but inexpensive miniature sculpture.

As they are small pieces, papier-mâché egg cups do not take long to make, so you can do several in one go, though they will not be ready to decorate until the glue has completely dried. This takes about a day.

Being made of papier mâché, these egg cups are not washable, but if you give them a final coat of tough polyurethane varnish you will be able to wipe them clean. Alternatively, tuck a small piece of linen into the egg cups to protect them from drips.

ABOVE THIS PAPIER-MÂCHÉ EGG CUP HAS BEEN FINELY DECORATED WITH GOUACHE PAINTS AND PEN LINES.

MATERIALS
Sheet of corrugated cardboard,
20cm x 18cm /8in x 7in
Sticky tape
Newspaper and PVA
China egg cup for mould
Vaseline
White emulsion
Gouache paints
Polyurethane varnish
Scalpel and scissors

1. USING A SCALPEL AND THE TEMPLATE ON PAGE 124 AS A GUIDE, CUT TWO STAND SHAPES AND THREE RECTANGLES 6CM/2½IN BY 5CM/2IN FOR THE BASE.

2. FIX THE STAND SHAPES ABOUT 2CM/¾IN APART ON ONE RECTANGLE BASE USING STICKY TAPE. STACK THE OTHER TWO RECTANGLES UNDER THIS AND STICK IN POSITION TO GIVE DEPTH TO THE BASE. COMPLETELY COVER THE STAND AND BASE WITH SMALL NEWSPAPER STRIPS USING PVA GLUE.

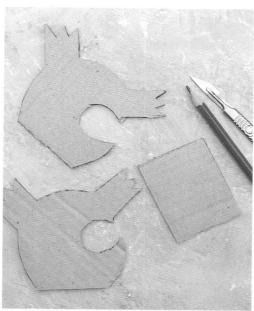

3. COAT THE INSIDE OF A CHINA EGG CUP WITH VASELINE THEN PASTE FOUR LAYERS OF NEWSPAPER STRIPS TO THE INSIDE. WHEN COMPLETELY DRY, REMOVE THE PAPIER-MÂCHÉ SHELL FROM THE EGG CUP MOULD. TRIM THE EDGES INTO PETAL SHAPES USING SCISSORS.

4. GLUE THE EGG CUP TO THE STAND, THEN COVER THE WHOLE PIECE WITH ONE MORE LAYER OF PASTED PAPER STRIPS. WHEN DRY, PAINT WITH WHITE EMULSION AND ALLOW TO DRY. DECORATE AND VARNISH.

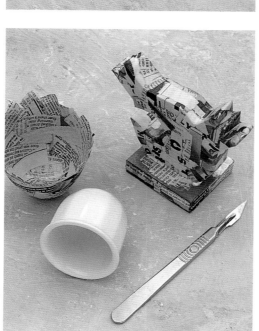

SPRINGTIME SWEATER

Inspired by American Indian art, this delightful jacket is designed to generous proportions for children aged three to ten and will not look out of place once Easter is over.

MATERIALS
Rowan handknit D.K.cotton:
5(6:7:8) x 50g balls, blue (A)
1(1:2:2) x 50g balls each of
peacock (B), yellow (C)
1(1:1:1) x 50g ball each of
mango (D), mustard (E), nut (F)
Pair each of 4mm(No 8) and 4½mm
(No 7) knitting needles
Cable needle
Open-ended zip fastener,
30(35:35:40)cm/12(14:14:16)in
5 white buttons, 8mm/¼in diameter
5 black buttons, 13mm/½in diameter
Bright orange embroidery thread

MEASUREMENTS
To fit age 3–4(5–6:7–8:9–10)
Actual chest size: 87(94:99:103)cm/
34½(37:39:40½)in
Length to shoulder: 38(41:43:47)cm/
15(16¼:17:18½)in
Sleeve seam: 24(28:32:36)cm/
9½(11:12½:14¼)in

RIGHT BUTTON EYES ADD TO THE APPEAL OF
THIS LIVELY SPRINGTIME SWEATER.

RIGHT A SINGLE BIRD FLIES
ACROSS THE SHOULDERS AT
THE BACK.

19 sts and 28 rows to 10cm/4in over st-st on 4½mm (No 7) needles

ABBREVIATIONS

beg: begin(ning); **cm:** centimetres; **cont:** continue; **foll:** following; **in:** inches; **inc:** increase; **K:** knit; **P:** purl; **patt:** pattern; **rem:** remaining; **rep:** repeat; **RS:** right side; **st(s):** stitch(es); **st-st:** stocking stitch; **tog:** together; **WS:** wrong side.

Figures in round brackets are for larger sizes. Repeat instructions in square brackets as given.

BACK

With 4mm (No 8) needles and B, cast on 78(86:90:94) sts. Work 2-colour rib, stranding colour not in use loosely across WS.

1st rib row (RS): K2B, [P2C, K2B] to end.
2nd rib row: P2B, [K2C, P2B] to end.
Rep 1st and 2nd rib rows 3(4:4:5) times more, inc one st at each end of last row for 1st size only. 80(86:90:94) sts.
Change to 4½mm (No 7) needles.
Beg with a K row, cont in st-st.
Work 2(6:10:14) rows A and 2 rows D.
Next row: K2(0:0:0)B, 4(5:3:5)C, [4B, 4C] to last 10(9:7:9) sts, K4B, 4(5:3:5)C, 2(0:0:0)B.
Next row: P2(0:0:0)B, 4(5:3:5)C, [4B, 4C] to last 10(9:7:9) sts, P4B, 4(5:3:5)C, 2(0:0:0)B.
Work 2 rows D and 52(52:54:56) rows A.

Work bird motif from chart for back. Use separate small balls of A and E for each colour area, twisting yarns tog at every colour change to link sts.
1st row (RS): K15(18:20:22)A, reading chart from right to left, K46 sts of row 1 of chart, K19 (22:24:26)A.
2nd row: P19(22:24:26)A, reading chart from left to right, P46 sts of row 2 of chart, P15(18:20:22)A.
Cont in this way until all 28 rows of chart have been completed.
Work 4(6:8:10) rows A.
Cast off loosely.

LEFT FRONT

With 4mm (No 8) needles and B, cast on 38(42:42:46) sts.
Rib 8(10:10:12) rows as back, inc 2 sts evenly across last rib row on 3rd size only. 38(42:44:46) sts.
Change to 4½mm (No 7) needles.
Beg with a K row, cont in st-st.
Work 2(6:10:14) rows A and 2 rows D.
Next row: K2(0:0:2)C, 4(2:4:4)B, [4C, 4B] to end.
Next row: P[4B, 4C] to last 6(2:4:6) sts, P4(2:4:4)B, 2(0:0:2)C.
Work 2 rows D and 2(2:6:10) rows A.
Cont in patt from chart for fronts, reading odd-numbered K rows from right to left and even-numbered P rows from left to right. Use separate small balls of yarn for each colour area, twisting yarns tog at every colour change to link sts.
Commence neck shaping on row 73 of chart, as indicated.

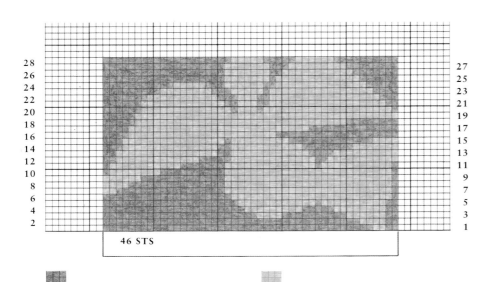

46 STS

A   E

ABOVE CHART FOR BACK.

When all 82 rows of chart have been completed, work 0(2:2:2) rows straight in A. Cast off rem 28 (32:34:36) sts.

RIGHT FRONT

Work to match left front, reading each of the two-coloured rows between D stripes from end to beg to reverse colours. When working from chart, read odd-numbered K rows from left to right and even-numbered P rows from right to left to reverse motifs and shaping.

CABLE PANEL

Worked in A over centre 8 sts of sleeves.
1st row (RS): P2, K4, P2.

2nd row: K2, P4, K2.
3rd row: P2, slip next 2 sts on to cable needle and hold at back, K2 then K2 sts from cable needle, P2.
4th row: As 2nd row.
5th row: As 1st row
6th row: As 2nd row.
7th row: P2, slip next 2 sts on to cable needle and hold at front, K2 then K2 sts from cable needle, P2.
8th row: As 2nd row. These 8 rows form patt for cable panel.

SLEEVES

With 4mm (No 8) needles and B, cast on 34(38:38:42) sts.
Rib 8(8:10:10) rows as back.
Change to 4½mm (No 7) needles.
Cont in A.
1st row(RS): K13(15:15:17), work 8 sts of 1st row of cable panel, K13

(15:15:17).
2nd row: P13(15:15:17), work 8 sts of 2nd row of cable panel, P13 (15:15:17).
Work a further 2(2:4:4) rows as set, working appropriate rows of cable panel at centre.
**Next row: K13(15:15:17)D, work 8 sts of cable panel in A, K13 (15:15:17)D.
Next row: P13(15:15:17)D, work 8 sts of cable panel in A, P13 (15:15:17)D**.
Next row: K0(1:1:3)C, 3(4:4:4)B, 4C, 4B, 2C, work 8 sts of cable panel in A, 2C, 4B, 4C, 3(4:4:4)B, 0(1:1:3)C.
Next row: P0(1:1:3)C, 3(4:4:4)B, 4C, 4B, 2C, work 8 sts of cable panel in A, 2C, 4B, 4C, 3(4:4:4)B, 0(1:1:3)C.
Rep from ** to ** once.
Keeping cable panel correct, cont in A, inc one st at each end of next and every foll 2nd(2nd:2nd:3rd) row until there are 64(56:48:72) sts, then on every foll 3rd(3rd:3rd:4th) row until there are 70(78:82:86) sts.
Cont straight until sleeve measures 24(28:32:36)cm/9½(11:12½:14¼) in from beg, ending with a WS row.
Saddle shaping: Cast off 31(35:37:39) sts at beg of next 2 rows. Cont in cable patt on rem 8 sts until saddle extension fits along cast off edge of front. Cast off.

FRONT BORDERS

With RS facing, 4mm (No 8) needles and B, pick up and K 78(82:86:94) sts evenly along front edge.

Beg with a 2nd rib row, rib 5 rows as at beg of back.
With B, cast off evenly knitwise.

NECKBAND

Sew sides of saddle extensions to cast-off edge of fronts and to 28(32:34:36) sts at each end of cast-off edge of back.
With RS facing, 4mm (No 8) needles and B, pick up and K90 (94:94:94) sts evenly around neck.
Beg with a 2nd rib row, rib 7 rows as at beg of back.
With B, cast off evenly knitwise.

TO MAKE UP

Join cast-off sts of saddle shaping to sides of back and fronts. Join side and sleeve seams. Sew in zip fastener. Using bright orange thread, embroider beaks and feet on to birds in satin stitch and back stitch. With A, embroider a line of back stitch to divide hare's ears. For eyes, place white button on top of black button and stitch together on to hares and birds.

RIGHT CHART FOR FRONT

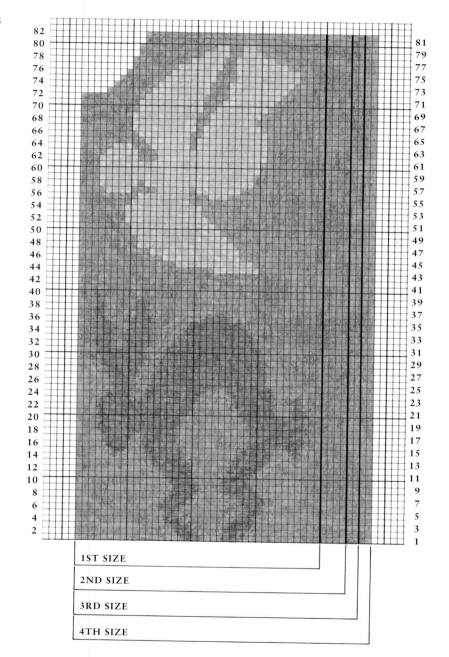

F

E

A

1ST SIZE

2ND SIZE

3RD SIZE

4TH SIZE

EASTER APPLIQUÉ

Spring sunshine at Easter holds the promise of weeks of fine weather. It is the time when thoughts turn from heavy winter overcoats to something altogether lighter, and a special family celebration at Easter offers the perfect opportunity to dress up in a new spring outfit that can last the summer through.

For children, appliqué is a charming and fun way to give the simplest of garments an instant designer look. The running hare and spring flowers in this design are cheerful Easter motifs, perfect for the special day, but they will not make the clothes look out of place at other times, even in the height of summer. Either make a new outfit, such as this delightful gingham pinafore, incorporating the motifs, or use the motifs to transform a manufactured garment. Alternatively stitch designs on to a band of fabric and sew as a panel on to a skirt, the side of a jacket, or even use to lengthen a little girl's skirt. While this gingham pinafore has a wonderful old-fashioned charm, the hares and flowers would also look stunning on more casual clothes, such as a pair of brightly coloured canvas dungarees, or even denims.

Almost any fabric can be used for appliqué, but the motifs are much easier to handle if they are cut from a robust, tightly woven material, which is more likely to lie flat as you work.

WORKING THE APPLIQUÉ

MATERIALS
Child's garment
Fabric remnants
Thin card
Tracing paper
Sewing machine
Embroidery scissors

First, make the template for the motif to be appliquéd. Using tracing paper and a soft lead pencil, trace off the shape (see page 124). Cut it out and place on thin card. Draw round this and cut out the card shape. Check the shape against the original and adjust if necessary. Place the template on the right side of the fabric you wish to use for the motif and carefully draw round it with a soft lead pencil. Cut out the shape allowing an extra 5mm/¼in all round. Place the fabric motif on the right side of the garment and tack it in position, across the middle, to ensure it lies flat. Following the pencil line, machine straight stitch all round the motif shape then, using very sharp scissors, carefully trim the motif as close as possible to the stitching. Set the machine to close zigzag stitch and restitch round the motif covering both the line of straight stitching and the raw edge.

ABOVE SIMPLE MACHINE EMBROIDERY ADDS DETAIL TO THE APPLIQUÉD MOTIFS.

RIGHT RUNNING HARES AND SPRING FLOWERS LEND AN EASTER FRESHNESS TO A LITTLE GIRL'S DRESS.

An alternative method to using straight stitch for the initial fixing is to use a fusing web, though this can be fiddly on small motifs. Lay the motif fabric on top of the fusing web and treat these layers as one. Using the template, draw out the motif and cut along the pencil line. Position the motif on the garment. Hold a warm iron on it to melt the fusing web adhesive. This bonds the motif to the garment. Finish with zigzag stitch to neaten the raw edge.

Decorate the appliqué with machine-embroidered stitches if you wish.

EASTER BONNETS

Traditionally, it was considered good luck to put on something new on Easter Sunday, which is perhaps where the custom of wearing Easter bonnets originated. The Easter Parade was an opportunity to wear something more decorative following the inclement winter weather when hats had to be of a more practical nature. Easter, being the official mark of spring, meant brighter colours and prettier, more extrovert styles were *de rigeur*. And, after church, there was just a chance to turn a few heads during the promenade.

Now that formal hats are worn less, it is much more likely to be the children who are putting on Easter bonnets. They welcome any opportunity to don a hat, and brightly coloured versions of Victorian styles are instantly appealing. Schools often organize Easter parades, giving parents the opportunity to re-live an unspoken Easter bonnet competition by making ever more imaginative hats for their children.

RIGHT A JOYFUL COLLECTION OF BONNETS THAT CHILDREN WILL LOVE TO WEAR FOR THE EASTER PARADE CAN BE ADAPTED FROM ONE BASIC SHAPE WITH THE SAME DECORATIONS USED AGAIN AND AGAIN TO DIFFERENT EFFECT.

CONSTRUCTING THE HATS

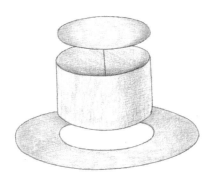

BASIC HAT PATTERN

A hat consists of two main parts: the brim and the crown which is made up of a side band and top piece. To make a hat, you first need to cut out a pattern. On paper, draw out the rectangular side band pattern: the length is the child's head measurement plus 2.5cm/1in; the depth is variable according to the particular design. Cut out the side band and shape it into a tube, overlapping by 2.5cm/1in at the back. On a large piece of paper, draw one circle the diameter of the tube for the top piece and a larger circle around it to make the brim. (A simple compass to draw large circles can be made by tying a pencil to one end of a piece of string the length of the radius, and fixing a drawing pin at the other end.) Cut out the circles.

When constructing the Easter hats, refer back to this basic pattern.

TOP HAT

MATERIALS
Plain paper for pattern
2 x A2 sheets of green card
A2 sheet of embossed red paper
A2 sheet of embossed green paper
A2 sheet of plain red paper
A2 sheet of plain green paper
Paper glue and scissors

Make a paper pattern for the side band to a depth of 25cm/8in. Divide this into eight equal sections with pencil lines (a). Cut along these lines, leaving the bottom edge joined. Place on a new piece of paper spreading the cut sections to create a 2cm/³⁄₄in gap between each at the top edge (b).

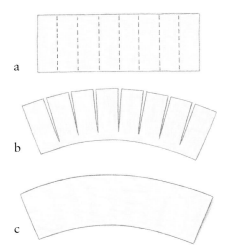

Draw round this shape and cut out (c). Bend the pattern into a tube and cut out a top circle. Cut a 6cm/2½in-wide brim to fit the narrower end. Cut the hat from green card, using the pattern but adding 1.5cm/⅝in allowance at the top of the

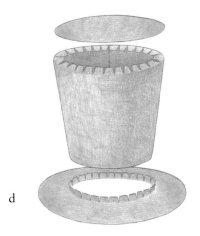

side band and at the inner edge of the brim. Score the card along the line of the original pattern and make V-cuts into the allowance to make tabs.

Construct the hat, gluing the tabs as shown (d). Cover the brim and top with red embossed paper and the side band with green.

Trim the top and brim with half rosettes and attach spiral concertinas to the brim in long loops (page 125).

POKE BONNET

MATERIALS
Plain paper for pattern
A2 sheet of pink card
A2 sheet of pink paper
A2 sheet of fuchsia paper
2m/2⅓yd satin ribbon
Paper glue and scissors

Make a paper pattern for the hatband. Divide the pattern into eight equal sections with pencil lines (a). Fold small darts along these lines to make the top edge shorter than the bottom (b). Place on a new piece of paper and cut out the new pattern. Trim the edge as shown (c). Cut a circle to fit the top diameter; and a 15cm/6in-wide brim to fit the lower .

Divide the brim into eight with

a

b

c

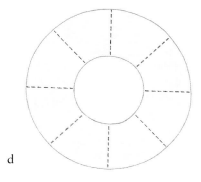

d

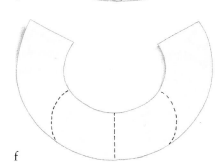

e

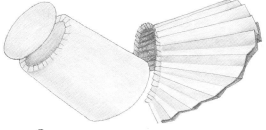

f

pencil lines (d). Pinch along these to make darts every 2.5cm/1in at the outer edge; tape the darts flat (e).

Cut through the pattern and cut out the front section as shown (f). To calculate this, use ⅔ of child's head measurement. Measure out half this figure on the inside curve to the left of centre and half to the right. Draw a curved line from these points to the front of the brim. Using the patterns, cut the side band and top piece from

pink card (allowing for tabs) and construct the crown. Cut a brim from each of the pink and fuchsia papers, adding an extra 1.5cm/⅝in to the shorter curve edge for tabs.

Fold the two brim pieces together in half across the middle, then make pleats outwards from here. Trim the

g

outer edge into points. Glue to the inside of the crown using the tabs .

Cut a rectangle of fuchsia paper 44cm/18in by the length of the radius and narrowly pleat it. Form it into a circle, stick the ends together and fix to the top piece. Make concertina rosettes (page 125), fix all round the base of the crown and add one to the top of the hat. Staple on ribbon ties.

ORIGAMI CHICKS AND DUCKS

Broods of brightly coloured paper chicks and ducklings perched along the window panes make delightful, easy-to-construct Easter decorations. They are classic designs in origami, the Japanese craft of paper-folding, which is believed to be more than 1000 years old. Even today, origami is a popular pastime in Japan, where it is used to make *noshis* (folded tokens) and elaborate gift packaging.

The secret behind the charm of these chicks and ducklings lies in the choice of paper. Sunshine yellow paper, some plain, some decorated with dog-tooth check, adds a seasonal feel. The less complicated forms of origami, like the two pieces shown here are not difficult to do, but newcomers to the craft may like to practise on plain paper first until they are familiar with all the folds.

Almost any paper can be used as long as it creases into crisp folds without stretching or tearing. Paper sold specially for origami is often coloured on one side and white on the other to add depth to the finished

LEFT OLDER CHILDREN CAN HELP WITH THE EASY-TO-FOLD ORIGAMI DUCKS AND CHICKS FOR AN ATTRACTIVE EASTER DISPLAY.

piece of work. In Japan, it is sometimes sold patterned on one side, plain on the other. The same effect can be achieved by sticking two pieces together back to back with spray adhesive or paper glue, and allowing them to dry completely before starting to fold.

Both the chick and the duck are made from squares, and it is important to cut the paper to shape accurately. To make a square from a rectangular piece of paper, place the paper on a hard surface with the narrow edge nearest you. Fold up the bottom right corner so the bottom edge of the paper lies exactly on top of the left-hand edge. Make a firm crease along the diagonal. The top layer of paper now forms a triangle. Fold the underneath projecting paper along the edge of the triangle. Crease. Cut along the crease. For full folding instructions for the chick and duck, see pages 120-21.

Successful origami relies on accurate and firm folding and creasing. Work on a hard surface and, for crisp results, run the back of your thumbnail down each crease before going on to the next.

Sometimes, the paper is simply folded into place. At other times, it is pre-creased and opened up before the fold is made. It is important not to hurry these steps, as the pre-creasing means that when a more complicated fold is being made, every part falls neatly into the correct place.

S P R I N G
FLOWERS

Nothing can be a more dramatic manifestation of rebirth than the explosion of flowers around Easter time. Blooms burst from unpromising twigs and flowers push through bare earth in an exuberant show of colour that is never quite matched at any other time of the year. Celebrate nature's own New Year by gathering up a small part of the bounty to enjoy indoors.

CELEBRATION
GARLAND

An important festival in its own right, Easter is a natural time to celebrate any new beginning and is often chosen as a time for more personal rejoicing. Weddings and christenings are especially popular at this time and warrant lavish floral decorations. Garlands are a hallmark of welcome and celebration; festoons of flowers say that a person or occasion merits the unsparing best of everything.

Garlands are usually made up using cut flowers and are normally expected to last only a day or two. To look fresh through the Easter holiday, however, requires a more lasting beauty. The garland shown here has been made up with potted plants. This altogether more sensitive way of using flowers allows the garland to be dismantled once the blooms are over and the individual plants to be planted out in the garden ready to flower again next year. Pansies and primroses were chosen because they are hardy right through spring and are easy to find, whether Easter is early or late.

Each season has its own predominant colours, so the secret behind

LEFT A FESTOON OF SPRING FLOWERS, IN JOYFUL YELLOWS AND GOLDS, MARKS THE SEASON'S CELEBRATIONS.

LEFT PAINTED EGGS ADD EASTER'S
TOUCH TO A SPRING GARLAND.

CONSTRUCTING THE GARLAND

MATERIALS
Small potted plants, about 6-10
per 30cm/12in of garland
Chicken wire the length of
garland and 2½ times
the width of shelf
60-80 florists' stub wires
(0.9mm/20 gauge)
Small terracotta pots, 2 per
30cm/12in of garland
Black plastic bin liners
Sphagnum moss

giving a garland a springtime personality is to commission nature to choose the shades.

Instead of dipping into the extensive palette of cultivated primrose colours, this garland has been based on the simple shades of the woodland variety. Violas and pansies have been added giving a whole range of subtle yellows from an almost papery off-white through butter and deep golds, softening to apricot and peach tones. With the addition of just one or two pansies in old rose shades, the garland takes on an enchanting Victorian feel.

To give the garland extra form, the primroses have been planted in old terracotta pots, their soft tones blurred further by the bloom of age complementing the peachy shades of the pansies.

Garlands must be in proportion to their surroundings: they will look mean if too small but will be overpowering if too large. For pleasing proportions, cut the chicken wire base to two-and-a-half times the width of the shelf, mantelpiece or lintel it is to rest on, and use plenty of plants for a lush look. Cover any exposed wire with moss.

Water plants and allow to drain. Pass a stub wire through the hole at the bottom of each pot, bend it in half bringing the ends together at the rim, then twist together and bend to form a hook. Plant a primrose in each pot.

For the remaining plants, cut the black plastic bin liners into squares large enough to hold a rootball. Tip each plant from its pot and place it in the centre of a square. Gather the plastic round the roots and loosely wind a stub wire around the neck to secure and enclose the rootball.

Roll and scrunch the chicken wire into a loose sausage shape and secure the bagged plants to this using stub wires bent in half in a hairpin shape. Fix a planted-up terracotta pot at intervals of about 15cm/6in. Finally, fill in the gaps with moss.

1. USE SMALL PLANTS RATHER THAN CUT FLOWERS FOR A GARLAND THAT WILL STAY FRESH ALL EASTER.

2. RESERVING THE PRIMROSES, 'REPOT' THE PLANTS IN PLASTIC, THEN FIX THESE TO THE CHICKEN WIRE.

3. WIRE UP AND PLANT TINY TERRACOTTA POTS WITH PRIMROSES TO LEND A STRUCTURED GARDEN FEEL.

4. ADD MOSS TO CONCEAL THE CHICKEN WIRE AND GIVE A WOODLAND QUALITY AND DEPTH TO THE FINISHED GARLAND.

SPRING'S BOUNTY

Nature seems to make a special effort in spring, putting on her most flamboyant apparel as if compensating for the long barren months of winter. The shades at this time of year are strong and clear: the vivid yellows of primroses, daffodils, cowslips and some tulips; the brilliant blues of hyacinths, bluebells and forget-me-nots; the deep magenta and pinks of hyacinths, cyclamen and many tulips. When set against the fleshy emerald green of spring leaves, these colours are somehow intensified.

Spring also specializes in abundance. Flowers crowd the countryside as if gathering for a festival, they increase their numbers in the garden unaided and they mass in the marketplace, all offering a plentiful supply of inexpensive blooms. And therein lies the secret of successful Easter displays. It is always better to buy armfuls of inexpensive flowers for a lavish show rather than settle for a paltry one.

LEFT AN EASTER GATHERING OF FLOWERS –
AURICULA, TULIPS, TINY RED SEDUM,
CYCLAMEN, PINK AND BLUE HYACINTHS,
CHERRY BLOSSOM, LENTEN ROSE
(HELLEBORE), NARCISSI, VIOLA, LILY OF THE
VALLEY, COWSLIPS, PRIMROSES,
FORGET-ME-NOTS AND WALLFLOWERS.

EASTER POSIES

The charm of a posy is that it evokes the romance of the Victorian age. During that time, well-dressed young ladies carried posies, coquettishly using them in courtship. The restrictions imposed by the segregation of boys and girls and men and women led to the development of a whole language of flowers. A gentleman would present his chosen lady with meaningful flowers; in reply, she would carry a relevant posy. It was a custom fraught with problems, however, as different dictionaries listed different meanings and, even when these were broadly in agreement, the courtship had to rely on the correct interpretation of subtle variations of meaning, often within one flower. A rose generally signified love, but to be presented with a yellow rose could mean jealousy, while, according to one dictionary, to receive the rose known as La France would be to receive an invitation to a moonlight meeting. To miss that message could irredeemably divert the course of a young lady's future.

Posies are most beautiful and authentic when composed of just one or two types of flower, mimicking the restrictions of the past that were imposed by the need to convey a clear, unambiguous message.

Alternatively, choose a closely matched colour scheme, such as woodland primroses with their enchanting cowslip cousins, or headily scented, pure white lilies of the valley with white forget-me-nots. Teaming differently coloured varieties of the same flower can be delightful, too. Delicate purple-and-yellow

LEFT ARRANGED AS BOUQUETS, SPRING FLOWERS CAN SIMPLY BE UNWRAPPED AND PUT STRAIGHT IN CONTAINERS.

RIGHT TRADITIONALLY, POSIES WERE POEMS PRESENTED WITH A SMALL BOUQUET OF FLOWERS, BUT HERE THE PLAIN PAPER REPRESENTS THE POEM AND THE FLOWERS CARRY THE MESSAGE INSTEAD.

violas look wonderful massed with plain yellow ones.

More sophisticated combinations could be achieved by combining the magenta of tiny woodland cyclamen and wild forget-me-nots in tones of sapphire and amethyst, or by mixing azure bluebells with orange, pink or red ranunculus.

MAKING UP A POSY

Before assembling the flowers, cut about 1cm/⅜in off the end of each stem using sharp secateurs, and put them in a bucket of warm water for a long drink.

The professional way to arrange flowers into a posy is to cross the stems, which gives each flower the space it needs without being crushed, while making the bunch look more generous. This simple idea needs practice, however. One trick is to form one hand into a 'vase' by making a circle with fingers and thumb, then 'arrange' the flowers in it. The finished posy can then be wrapped – plain paper shows off the flowers best – ready for giving.

THE LANGUAGE OF SPRING FLOWERS

Anenome – *Forgiveness*
Auricula – *Painting*
Bluebell – *Reliability*
Cowslip – *Thoughtfulness*
Cyclamen – *Timidity, shyness*
Daffodil – *Respect*
Forget-me-not – *True love*
Hyacinth – *Playfulness*
Lily – *Purity*
Lily of the valley – *Return of happiness*

Narcissus – *Egotism*
Pansy – *Thoughts*
Pink – *Pure love*
Primrose – *Young one*
Ranunculus – *Radiant charm*
Tulip (red) – *I love you*
Tulip (yellow) – *Hopeless love*
Tulip (variegated) – *Beautiful eyes*
Violet – *Humility*
Wallflower – *Faithful against the odds*

THE LOVELINESS OF LILIES

Breathtakingly beautiful and symbolic of purity, tall white lilies are traditionally used as altar decorations at Easter time.

With their sculptural form and sweet, heady perfume, radiant *longiflorum* lilies make an elegant focus for this beguiling outdoor scene. Although bought as cut flowers, these lilies have been arranged as if they are growing outdoors in a mossy bed that is backed by a twiggy garden frame interwoven with trailing clematis. Terracotta pots of white scilla, delicate lily of the valley and old-fashioned, dusty-toned auricula have been added along with a group of tiny bantams' eggs, a generously sized goose egg and a handmade nest containing quails' eggs. The finished arrangement evokes all that is delightful about a gentle, clear spring day – fragrance, delicate flowers and burgeoning new life, symbolized by the eggs.

The inherent elegance of lilies makes them easy to arrange. Just two stems placed in a tall vase create a beautiful still life without the need for added foliage.

The lily has always been regarded as a flower of unmatched loveliness. Worthy of kings and emperors, it appeared in paintings on the walls of Cretan palaces over three thousand years ago, and inspired bronze capitals on columns in Solomon's palace. The New Testament exhorts us to 'Consider the lilies. Even Solomon in all his glory was not arrayed like one of these'.

Botanists believe that the lily so revered in the past for its beauty was the Madonna lily, native to Palestine and sought after for its rarity value, possibly because it is notoriously hard to grow. This same lily has appeared in Christian art through the centuries, symbolizing purity and chastity. In pictures of the Annunciation, Gabriel is sometimes shown carrying a lily, and Joseph also holds one in his hand to signify Mary's virginity.

For hundreds of years, the hard-to-please Madonna lily was the only one available to gardeners, but new varieties have now been discovered, often at great cost. When the young English botanist, Ernest Henry Wilson discovered the exquisite regal lily (*Lilium regale*) on the borders of Tibet at the turn of the century, he was determined to send a substantial supply back to the Arnold Arboretum, his Boston employers. On one expedition, falling rock smashed his leg as he was crossing a narrow gorge and he had to lie still as the rest of the party, including 50 mules, stepped over him. Thankfully, his leg was saved, and his prize was 7,000 bulbs to send home.

Until recently, Easter lilies were grown mainly in Holland and Belgium for export, and they used to be flown across the Atlantic specially for the springtime celebrations. They have now become so popular in the United States of America that they are grown on the northern Pacific coast, Florida, Louisiana and Texas for the occasion.

An alternative to using cut flowers for an Easter arrangement is to use growing lilies which can then be either potted or transferred to the garden to bloom year after year, once the indoor display is over its best.

With the introduction of new hardy hybrids, lilies have shrugged off their old reputation for being difficult to grow. Many will flower every spring or summer with little help. Buying a variety that suits your soil (some hate lime) and making sure it is comfortably bedded down are the main priorities. While some species develop feeding roots at the bottom of the bulb, others have them above it and need to be planted at least three times the depth of the bulb. Planted in humus-rich soil in a sand-lined pocket, to prevent rotting and slug attack, they should thrive with very little attention.

LEFT THE GREENY-WHITE TRUMPETS OF THE LONGIFLORUM LILY MAKE A STUNNING FOCUS FOR AN ELEGANT EASTER DISPLAY.

BASKETS OF FLOWERS

An Easter basket of flowering plants makes a precious gift because, once they have finished blooming, they can be planted in a special corner of the garden as a memento.

Despite their delicate appearance, many spring flowers are easy to grow on, eagerly spreading and naturalizing over the years.

With flowering bulbs, the success of future blooming relies on allowing plenty of sunshine to be absorbed into the dying leaves. At this rather untidy-looking stage, the bulb baskets can be tucked into a secluded corner to soak up the sun unnoticed. Only once the leaves have shrivelled are the bulbs ready to plant out. Where spring bulbs provide small challenge to any gardener, some of the other spring flowers are a little more delicate. Pansies, for example, will probably provide a reasonable show for only one more season.

Fragile-looking auriculas, on the other hand, are quite hardy, though they will need a little cossetting for the first year. Simply repot and feed them well. By the second year, they can be planted out in a hole lined with sanding grit to protect them from marauding slugs. From then on, they should provide a lively display year after year.

1. WITH THEIR DUSTY SHADES AND TEXTURE OF DAMASK, AURICULAS ARE REGAINING THE POPULARITY OF THEIR VICTORIAN HEYDAY.

2. PURE WHITE BLOOMS AND A BACKGROUND OF RICH GREEN LEAVES, MAKE LILY OF THE VALLEY ONE OF THE MOST BEAUTIFUL SPRING BULBS.

3. WHO COULD RESIST THE CHARMS OF THESE MERRY, DOUBLE YELLOW TULIPS PRESENTED IN A GREEN GALVANIZED BUCKET?

4. THE SOFT PURPLE SHADES OF THE CHEQUERED SNAKE'S HEAD FRITILLARY LOOK WONDERFUL NEXT TO THE WARM TONES OF OLD TERRACOTTA.

5. NEAT LITTLE VIOLAS MAKE A DELIGHTFUL PARTNER TO A TRUG FULL OF HEARTSEASE, THEIR WILDER SISTERS.

6. THE ADDITION OF MOSS AND TINY RED SEDUM TRANSFORMS AN ENAMEL BATH CONTAINING CRIMSON TULIPS.

BLOSSOM TREE

Clouds of blossom bursting from bare twigs are the epitome of spring – life emerging from the apparent death of the winter tree. A lovely idea is to bring in some bare branches a few weeks before Easter then watch the blooms burgeon and clamour for space on the laden boughs. Although this was one of Queen Alexandra's favourite Easter rituals, it is not a particularly common custom in Britain. The Easter tree is much more likely to be seen in continental Europe or in America. In Germany, silver birch branches are traditionally brought indoors, the shimmering bark and tiny, unfurling lettuce-green leaves providing a delightful framework on which to hang painted wooden eggs.

The idea can be copied using many kinds of branch: sculptural larch, its bare limbs trimmed all winter long with miniature cones that are later joined by tiny bunches of vivid green needles and tufts of crimson blooms; varieties of pussy willow, ranging from those that bear neat, silky, silver cushions to those with fatter, more flamboyant flowers in shades of burnt rose; or birch and hazel branches cloaked in cascades of greeny-yellow catkins that sway in the wind.

For sheer abundance, nothing can match delicately scented fruit blossoms, which dance in the breeze like a myriad ballerinas. These range from the purest white pear through pink-budded apple that pales as it opens, to the generous blush-pink of ornamental cherry and even stronger shades on some of the cultivated crab apple trees.

Market stalls and florists' shops are a good source for spring branches of all types. If cutting from the garden, use sharp secateurs and cut at an angle away from and just above a new outward-budding node. This way, there will be less damage to the branch, and it will be encouraged to thicken out over the summer.

It is easy to make a stunning display from any size of spring branches as there is so little arrangement involved. Very often just three or four branches are enough to create a pleasing balance. Cut to size with sharp secateurs, they can be supported by a ball of chicken wire, scrunched to shape and fitted into a sturdy container. Chicken wire is a better choice for anchoring branches than florists' foam, which is soon broken up by the thick woody stems. Wire also allows for slight movement, which creates a much more natural overall effect.

Terracotta urns and garden pots are a good choice of container for this kind of display as they offer a refreshing outdoor look, as if a corner of the garden has been brought inside.

Easter trees need only very simple decoration. Eggs of all types are an obvious but nonetheless pleasing option, their shape providing a smooth, uncluttered foil for the dense blossom. Hens' eggs can be dyed, painted, engraved or gilded, before being hung on the tree, or for a natural look, you can choose some of the less familiar domestic fowls' eggs such as tiny speckled quails' eggs, bantams' eggs, duck eggs in shades of delicate greeny-blue, or generously proportioned goose eggs. Prepare them by making a pin prick at each end, then blowing out the contents and thoroughly rinsing with warm water. To hang the eggs on the tree, make a loop at one end of a length of heavy gauge fuse wire or florists' silver wire and thread a ribbon through this. Feed the other end through the egg. Trim the wire and turn up the protruding end to support the bottom of the egg.

Another idea is to deck out Easter trees with small gifts. These could be trios of tiny, foil-wrapped chocolate eggs, perhaps parcelled in a twist of cellophane and tied with raffia; miniature filled baskets; or Easter biscuits looped through with ribbon.

RIGHT CLOUDS OF WHITE PEAR BLOSSOM HUNG WITH, PALE BLUE DUCK EGGS ON DIAPHANOUS RIBBON CELEBRATE THE FRESHNESS OF SPRING.

MOSS HARE

This engaging moss hare stands 45cm/18in high including ears, and can be made for the Easter celebrations, but if well looked after he will last a lot longer. Kept indoors and given a weekly spray of water, he could be around for months; outdoors, he needs to be kept in the shade and protected, just like a real hare, from predators such as cats, dogs and young children!

It is worthwhile searching out Italian moss which keeps its colour for a lot longer than the common sphagnum moss – months compared with weeks. Also, the natural contrast between the deep green top side and the brown roots, can be put to great effect on the ears.

MATERIALS
Chicken wire,
1m x 30cm/39 x 12in
Aproximately 40 florists'
stub wires
(0.71mm/22 gauge)
Sphagnum moss for filling
Italian moss for covering
2 toymakers' teddy eyes and 1
nose, or small dried flowers
Twigs for whiskers
1m/39in wired ribbon

LEFT THE INSPIRATION FOR THIS AMIABLE EASTER HARE IS ROOTED IN EIGHTEENTH-CENTURY GARDEN TOPIARY.

1. SHAPE THE HARE'S BODY PARTS BY BENDING CHICKEN WIRE AROUND SPHAGNUM MOSS. MAKE THE BODY 20CM/8IN HIGH WITH A 55CM/21½ IN CIRCUMFER-ENCE. THE HEAD IS EGG-SHAPED, 15CM/6IN LONG. THE LIMBS HAVE A CIRCUMFERENCE OF 10CM/4IN; LEGS 15CM/6IN LONG AND ARMS 10CM/4IN LONG.

2. CAREFULLY COVER EACH BODY PART WITH ITALIAN MOSS PINNED IN PLACE WITH SHORT STUB WIRES BENT HAIRPIN STYLE.

3. PIN THE BODY PARTS TOGETHER USING FULL-LENGTH STUB WIRES BENT HAIRPIN STYLE.

4. FOR THE EARS CUT TWO PIECES OF ITALIAN MOSS 15 X 10CM/6 X 4IN. WITH THE BROWN SIDE OF THE MOSS FACING FORWARDS AND GATHERED TOGETHER AT THE BASE, FIX THE EARS TO THE HEAD WITH BENT STUB WIRES. FIX ON THE EYES AND NOSE USING STUB WIRES. FINISH OFF WITH TWIGGY WHISKERS AND A WIRED RIBBON BOW.

DRIED-FLOWER NEST

While eggs abound at Easter, the image of the nest is largely ignored. Yet this symbol of new life, being both womb and cradle for baby birds, is a wonderful way of presenting decorated or chocolate eggs. Or leave the eggs in their natural state and make the nest into a delightful frame, mimicking nature.

The nest's appeal evokes the sense of discovering something private. In the wild, nests are built in the most inaccessible, secret places and the chances of finding one complete with eggs are rare, since even in the few weeks that nests are occupied, there is usually a parent bird in attendance. Happening upon one brings with it an almost mystical sense of discovery.

This thrill led to the popular and highly destructive Victorian hobby of nest and egg collection. Thankfully, the resulting decimation of the native bird population has been halted and today, disturbing either eggs or nest is outlawed.

LEFT FILLED WITH DAINTY BANTAMS' EGGS, THIS ENCHANTING NEST, FASHIONED FROM DRIED GRASSES AND FLOWERS, CAN BE STORED AWAY AFTER EASTER, AND USED AGAIN YEAR AFTER YEAR.

This nest is made from dried mosses, grasses and leaves which have been woven round a chicken wire base, then decorated with just a few dried flowers – delicate yellow lady's mantle (*alchemilla*) and everlasting strawflowers (*Helichrysum bracteatum*) in several shades of red through to oranges and yellows.

The nest is most successful and makes more of a statement when generously sized with just a few eggs shyly gathered in the bottom. Little bantams' eggs like the ones here, picked up from a local farm, offer far more interest than standardized supermarket hens' eggs which are uniform in size and colour. Without commercial restrictions, the bantams' eggs come in a more natural range from almost pure white to pale tan. Try your butcher or farm shop for a wider choice of eggs. Perhaps more suggestive of wild eggs are dainty, randomly spotted quails' eggs. For larger displays, look for duck eggs, which come in a range of delicate greeny-blue, or even creamy-coloured goose eggs.

Mounted with florists' wire on to a V-shaped branch of contorted willow, the nest is given structure and enough support to stand unaided on a table top. If Easter is late and the weather is fine, it may even be possible to find early blossoming contorted willow – the dancing yellow catkins will add life to the arrangement.

TOPIARY EGGS

Moss and floral eggs set in simple terracotta pots make enchanting Easter decorations, perfect for table, bedside or windowsill. Like miniature garden topiary, they offer an architectural discipline for a charming, unfussy display. The moss version is a witty copy of real topiary, the deep bun moss texture mimicking the density of clipped box; though unlike the real thing, it does not grow and so keeps its neat tailored shape. The floral egg is quite different: as each bloom opens, so the shape evolves, becoming a living sculpture.

Keep the floral eggs fresh by pouring water into the top, letting it soak into the florists' foam, and then gently spraying the blooms. This needs to be done every day.

The moss eggs will last longer if you use bun moss which retains its colour well. Choose the cushioned bun-like pieces for their variation in shade to give a richer look, then jigsaw them together over soaked florists' foam and fix in position with stub wires bent hairpin style. Keep the finished egg fresh with a daily spray of water.

RIGHT DENSE MOSS AND SMALL, FRAGRANT BLOOMS SUCH AS PINKS ARE IDEAL FOR MAKING EGG-SHAPED ARRANGEMENTS.

FASHIONING A FLORAL EGG

MATERIALS
Terracotta pot
Black plastic bin liner
Block of florists' foam
Sticky florists' tape
Stub wires
(0.71mm/22 gauge)
Approximately 24 miniature
spray roses
Bun moss

Before starting, thoroughly soak the florists' foam and condition the flowers by cutting off the ends of the stems at an angle using secateurs. Soak them in tepid water for several hours or overnight. You can leave the terracotta pot as it is or paint it to complement the scheme.

Line the pot with plastic, then cut the florists' foam into pieces and build up into an egg shape. Tape it into position in the pot and add a little moss round the rim of the pot.

Form 'ribbons' of bun moss to divide the egg into quarters vertically and fix these in place with stub wires bent to form a hairpin shape.

Using secateurs, trim the rose stems to about 5cm/2in then push these into the foam to make a compact arrangement completely covering the exposed foam.

1. A TERRACOTTA POT, FLORISTS' FOAM, BLACK PLASTIC AND FLORAL TAPE PROVIDE THE FOUNDATIONS.

2. CAREFULLY BUILD UP THE FLORISTS' FOAM INTO AN EGG SHAPE, THEN TAPE IT IN POSITION.

3. QUARTER THE EGG WITH BUN MOSS, FIXING IT IN PLACE WITH BENT STUB WIRES.

4. THE TINIEST SPRAY ROSES, MAKE THE MOST SUCCESSFUL EGGS AS LARGER ONES MAY DISTORT THE SHAPE AS THEY OPEN.

E A S T E R
FEASTS

Following the lenten fast, Easter is
a time of feasting. Time to enjoy
scrumptious eggy breakfasts laid
out on decorative seasonal tables,
countless teatime treats and delicious main meals of juicy meats
delicately flavoured with spring
herbs and accompanied by tender
young vegetables.

LEFT FESTIVE SAFFRON BREAD WITH ITS
FRESH YELLOW CRUMB.

EASTER BREADS

CORNISH SAFFRON BREAD

Saffron has been used in English cooking for centuries being most popular in Cornwall and Essex, both famous for their saffron breads. At one time the saffron grown at Saffron Walden was esteemed throughout the world and saffron buns were made at Easter time instead of the more traditional hot cross buns.

Makes 1 loaf

300ml/½ pint milk
1 tsp saffron strands
30g/1oz fresh yeast, or
15g/½oz dried yeast
450g/1lb strong plain flour
1 tsp salt
170g/6oz butter, cut into pieces
85g/3oz caster sugar
170g/6oz currants
55g/2oz candied peel, finely diced
finely grated rind of ½ lemon
vegetable oil and extra butter for greasing

Put the milk in a small saucepan and bring to the boil. Remove from the heat, sprinkle in the saffron and leave to stand for 30 minutes.

Reheat the milk just to lukewarm, then take off the heat. Crumble the fresh yeast in a bowl and cream it to a smooth liquid with the saffron-flavoured milk. Stir in 4 tbsp of the flour, then cover and leave the mixture for about 20 minutes to become foamy. If using dried yeast, mix the granules with the saffron-flavoured milk and 1 tsp of the sugar and set aside, covered, for about 15 minutes until frothy.

Sift the remaining flour with the salt, then rub in the butter until the mixture resembles fine crumbs. Stir in the sugar. Add the yeast liquid and mix to form a soft dough.

Turn out the dough on to a lightly floured surface and knead for about 10 minutes until the dough is smooth and elastic. Knead in the currants, candied peel and lemon rind. Shape the dough into a ball, place it inside an oiled polythene bag and tie the bag closed. Leave the dough to rise in a warm place for about 1 hour, or until doubled in size.

Meanwhile, grease a 20cm/8in round cake tin with butter. Turn out the risen dough on to a lightly floured surface. Knock back and knead the dough lightly, then shape it into a ball to fit the tin. Put it into the tin, pressing down well. Cover and leave to rise in a warm place for about 45 minutes, or until the dough just reaches the top of the tin. Pre-heat the oven to 180C/350F/Gas 4.

Bake for 45-60 minutes until golden brown and the loaf sounds hollow when tapped underneath. Transfer the bread to a wire rack to cool completely. Serve in slices spread with butter.

HOT CROSS BUNS

Small, spiced yeast buns have long been popular in Britain. Hot cross buns are made traditionally for Good Friday with the sign of the cross on top. If you do not want to make the flour and water paste to form the cross, you can use ready-made short-crust pastry cut into thin strips.

Makes 12

30g/1oz fresh yeast, or
15g/½oz dried yeast
300ml/½ pint milk, lukewarm
450g/1lb strong plain flour
1 tsp salt
1 tsp ground mixed spice
1 tsp ground cinnamon
1 tsp grated nutmeg
55g/2oz light muscovado sugar
55g/2oz butter, melted
1 egg, beaten
55g/2oz currants
55g/2oz sultanas
55g/2oz cut mixed peel
vegetable oil for greasing

TO FINISH
55g/2oz plain flour, plus extra for dusting
3 tbsp caster sugar

Crumble the fresh yeast in a bowl and cream it to a smooth liquid with the milk. Stir in 4 tbsp of the strong plain flour, then cover and leave the mixture for about 20 minutes to become foamy. If using dried yeast, mix the granules with the milk and 1 tsp of the sugar and set aside, covered, for about 15 minutes until frothy.

Sift together the remaining strong plain flour, salt, spices and sugar. Stir the butter and egg into the yeast mixture, then add to the spiced flour and mix together – the dough should be fairly soft.

Turn out the dough on to a lightly floured surface and knead for about 10 minutes until it is smooth and elastic. Knead in the fruit and mixed peel. Shape the dough into a ball, place it inside an oiled polythene bag and tie the bag closed. Leave the dough to rise in a warm place for 45-60 minutes, or until doubled in size. Meanwhile, heavily flour two baking trays.

Turn out the risen dough on to a lightly floured surface. Knock back and knead the dough lightly for 1 minute. Divide the dough into 12 pieces and shape each one into a smooth bun. Arrange the buns well apart on the baking trays and leave to

rise, covered, in a warm place for 20-30 minutes until doubled in size.

Meanwhile, pre-heat the oven to 190C/375F/Gas 5. To finish the buns, mix the plain flour with 4 tbsp water to form a thick paste. Using a piping bag fitted with a fine, plain nozzle, pipe a cross on each bun. Bake for about 20 minutes until the buns are golden brown and sound hollow when tapped underneath. Transfer to a wire rack.

Just before the buns are cooked, make the glaze. Heat the sugar and 4 tbsp water together in a small saucepan until dissolved, then bring to the boil. Immediately brush the hot buns with the glaze twice, then leave to cool completely. Serve the buns fresh with butter.

BELOW HOT CROSS BUNS ARE BELIEVED TO HAVE ORIGINATED AT ST ALBANS ABBEY TO WELCOME EASTER PILGRIMS.

GREEK SWEET EASTER BREAD
TSOUREKI

Easter is the most important feast time in Greece, and these sweet bread plaits (see page 99) are traditionally made for the celebrations. The red decorated eggs are a symbol of fertility and rebirth at the beginning of spring.

Makes 3 loaves

55g/2oz fresh yeast, or
30g/1oz dried yeast
125ml/4fl oz water, lukewarm
150g/5½oz sugar
225g/8oz butter
5 eggs
400ml/14fl oz milk, lukewarm
1.5kg/3½lb strong plain flour
vegetable oil for greasing
1 egg yolk
sesame seeds
6 hard-boiled eggs, dyed red
(see page 21)

Crumble the fresh yeast in a bowl and cream it to a smooth liquid with the water. Stir in 2 tbsp of the flour, then cover and leave the mixture for about 20 minutes to become foamy. If using dried yeast, mix the granules with the water and 1 tsp of the sugar and set aside, covered, for about 15 minutes until frothy.

Beat the butter and sugar in another large bowl until light and fluffy, then beat in the eggs, 1 at a time. Slowly pour in the milk and the yeast mixture, beating well. Gradually add the remaining flour and mix to form a soft dough.

Turn out the dough on to a lightly floured surface and knead for 10 minutes until smooth and elastic. Shape the dough into a ball, place it inside an oiled polythene bag and tie the bag closed. Leave the dough to rise in a warm place for at least 1 hour, or until doubled in size.

Turn out the risen dough on to a lightly floured surface. Knock back and knead the dough lightly for 1 minute. Return the dough to the oiled bag, tie closed and leave to rise again in a warm place for about 40 minutes until doubled in size. Meanwhile, oil two or three baking trays, depending on the size of the trays and how many shelves your oven has; if the trays are large enough you can bake two plaits on one tray.

Turn out the risen dough on to a lightly floured surface. Knock back the dough and divide it into nine equal pieces. Knead each piece until smooth, then roll into a strand about 50cm/20in long. Work with three strands at a time, keeping the remainder covered with a damp tea towel. Lightly wet each strand at one end and join together, then plait them together. Place the plaited loaf on a well-oiled baking tray. Continue to make two more loaves the same way.

Brush the loaves with the egg yolk mixed with 1 tbsp water and sprinkle generously with sesame seeds. Press 2 eggs into each loaf, cover with a clean tea towel and leave for a final rise in a warm place for about 40 minutes until the dough springs back easily when pressed. Meanwhile, pre-heat the oven to 190C/375F/Gas 5.

Bake the loaves for about 35 minutes until they are well browned and sound hollow when tapped underneath. Transfer to wire racks and leave to cool completely. The loaves will keep well wrapped in cling film at room temperature for a week. If you want to freeze any leftover loaves, remove the eggs first.

KULICH

This Russian sweet bread is traditionally made in a very tall mould, then iced to resemble a candle with the wax dripping down the sides. It is the custom to eat this with a rich mixture called *pashka* which includes curd cheese, soured cream and fruit. Well-scrubbed and dried coffee tins can be used instead of the authentic moulds which are difficult to find and also very expensive.

Makes 2 loaves

25g/¼oz fresh yeast, or
15g/½oz dried yeast
150ml/¼ pint milk, lukewarm
375g/13oz strong plain flour
55g/2oz raisins
55g/2oz candied peel, finely diced
2 tbsp vodka
115g/4oz butter, softened, plus extra

for greasing moulds
75g/2½oz caster sugar
½ tsp natural vanilla essence
4 egg yolks
¼ tsp salt
vegetable oil for greasing
30g/1oz blanched almonds, chopped

ICING AND DECORATION
1 tbsp lemon juice
150g/5oz icing sugar, sifted
candied fruit, to decorate

Crumble the fresh yeast into a bowl and cream it to a smooth liquid with the milk. Stir in 2 tbsp of the flour, then cover and leave the mixture for about 20 minutes to become frothy. If using dried yeast, mix the granules with the milk and 1 tsp of the sugar and set aside, covered, for about 15 minutes until frothy. Meanwhile, soak the raisins and candied peel in the vodka, leaving the bowl covered. Grease two clean 450g/1lb coffee tins (10cm/4in wide and 15cm/6in high) with butter.

Cream the butter with the sugar until light and fluffy, then add the vanilla essence and beat in the egg yolks, one at a time. Add this mixture with the remaining flour and the salt to the yeast mixture and beat to form a soft, smooth dough. Cover with oiled cling film and leave the dough to rise in a warm place for 1-1½ hours or until doubled in size.

Turn out the risen dough on to a lightly floured surface. Knock back

and lightly knead for about 1 minute, kneading in the almonds and soaked fruit. Divide the dough between the two tins, cover with oiled cling film and leave to rise in a warm place for about 40 minutes, or until the dough almost reaches the top of the tins. Meanwhile, pre-heat the oven to 200C/400F/Gas 6.

Bake the loaves for 15 minutes, then reduce the oven temperature to 180C/350F/Gas 4 and bake for a further 30 minutes until a skewer inserted in the centre comes out clean. Leave the loaves to cool in the tins until the tins are cool enough to handle, then unmould the loaves and transfer to wire racks to cool.

ABOVE HOT CROSS BUNS, MARKED WITH A CROSS TO COMMEMORATE THE CRUCIFIXION, AND KULICH, AN ICED RUSSIAN EASTER BREAD FLAVOURED WITH FRUIT SOAKED IN VODKA AND DECORATED WITH LEMON ICING.

Stir the lemon juice and 2 tbsp water into the icing sugar to make a thick icing. Cover the top of each loaf, allowing the icing to dribble down the sides. Decorate with candied fruit. The traditional way to serve *kulich* is to make horizontal slices, reserving the top slice as a lid. The second loaf can be kept for about a week, well wrapped in cling film. If it starts to dry out, however, it makes excellent toast.

EGG DISHES

SCRAMBLED EGGS IN THEIR SHELLS
Serves 4

8 free-range eggs
3 tbsp milk
salt and freshly ground black pepper
45g/1½oz unsalted butter
3 tbsp double cream
2 tbsp chopped fresh chervil or parsley

OPTIONAL GARNISHES
caviar
crumbled crispy bacon
chopped smoked salmon
chervil or flat-leaf parsley leaves

Very carefully remove a 'lid' from the pointed end of each egg using a small sharp knife. Place 6 of the eggs in a bowl. (The contents of the other 2 eggs are not needed for this recipe but their shells are!) Wash and dry the egg shells and place in egg cups.

Beat the eggs with the milk and plenty of salt and pepper.

Melt the butter in a non-stick saucepan and cook the eggs over gentle heat, stirring all the time until they are just beginning to set but are still liquid. Remove from the heat and keep stirring whilst you add the cream – the heat of the pan will continue cooking the eggs and the cream will give a rich creamy texture. Stir in the chervil or parsley.

Spoon the scrambled eggs into the prepared egg shells, garnish with caviar and herb leaves and serve at once with fingers of freshly buttered toast, or accompany with a bowl of caviar, bacon or smoked salmon.

SMOKED HADDOCK COCOTTES WITH SPINACH
Makes 4

600ml/1 pint milk
1 bay leaf
2 sprigs fresh thyme
450g/1lb smoked haddock fillet
150ml/¼ pint double cream
2 egg yolks
1 tbsp chopped fresh fennel or dill leaf
freshly ground black pepper
15g/½oz butter, plus extra for greasing
15g/½oz plain flour
55g/2oz Cheddar cheese, grated
4 tomatoes, sliced
4 sprigs fresh fennel or dill, to garnish

SPINACH
450g/1lb fresh baby spinach
45g/1½oz butter
55g/2oz onion, finely chopped
ground nutmeg and salt

Put the milk, bay leaf and thyme in a large frying pan and bring to the boil. Add the smoked haddock and simmer for 3 minutes. Drain, reserving the

RIGHT A GOURMET BREAKFAST OF SMOKED HADDOCK COCOTTES WITH SPINACH AND SCRAMBLED EGGS GARNISHED WITH CAVIAR.

cooking liquid, then remove the skin and flake the fish, discarding any bones. Meanwhile, pre-heat the oven to 200C/400F/Gas 6.

Beat the cream and egg yolks with the fennel or dill leaf, then stir in the fish. Season generously with pepper. Transfer the mixture to four buttered ramekins (size 1), cover each with a piece of buttered foil and set in a roasting tin. Pour boiling water into the tin to come at least two-thirds of the way up the sides of the dishes. Bake for 20-25 minutes until just set. Remove the ramekins from the tin and leave for a few moments for the mixture to set firm.

While the ramekins are baking, make the sauce and prepare the spinach. To make the sauce, melt the butter in a small saucepan, then stir in the flour. Cook for about 1 minute, stirring, then stir in 300ml/½ pint of the reserved cooking liquid, a little at a time, until smooth and thickened, then simmer for 2-3 minutes. Stir in the grated cheese and season with pepper. Add a little more of the reserved liquid as necessary to give a pouring consistency.

To prepare the spinach, remove any coarse stalks and place the leaves in a large saucepan. Cover with boiling water and bring back to the boil. Drain immediately and squeeze out excess liquid by wrapping in a clean tea towel and twisting the ends in opposite directions. Melt the butter in a frying pan and sauté the onion

for 2-3 minutes until softened. Add the spinach and toss quickly until heated through. Season to taste with nutmeg, salt and pepper.

Arrange the spinach in a pile on each dinner plate. Top with a smoked fish cocotte and spoon a little sauce over each one. Garnish with tomato slices and a sprig of fennel or dill.

SMOKED SALMON AND QUAILS' EGG NESTS
Makes 6

12 quails' eggs
170g/6oz smoked salmon, cut into
thin strips

LEFT DELICATE QUAILS' EGGS IN A NEST OF SMOKED SALMON DRESSED IN A CREAM SAUCE.

RIGHT PICATOSTES ARE EQUALLY GOOD SOAKED IN A HONEY SYRUP AND SERVED WITH CUPS OF HOT CHOCOLATE.

POTATO CAKES
450g/1lb potato, peeled and
coarsely grated
2 egg yolks
2 tbsp plain flour
½ tsp salt
¼ tsp ground pepper
vegetable oil for frying

SAUCE
150ml/¼ pint fish stock
150ml/¼ pint double cream
55g/2oz cream cheese
2 tbsp chopped fresh chives
lemon juice
cayenne pepper
salt and freshly ground black pepper

Pre-heat the oven to 150C/300F/ Gas 2.

To make the potato cakes, wrap the coarsley grated potato in a clean tea towel and squeeze out the excess moisture. Mix with the remaining ingredients.

Heat a little oil in a large non-stick frying pan. Divide the potato mixture in six equal portions and spoon each portion into the pan, pressing it down firmly with the back of the spoon to flatten as much as possible – you might need to do this in two batches. Fry the potato cakes for 3-4 minutes on each side until crisp and golden at the edges. Drain well on kitchen paper. Keep warm in the oven.

To make the sauce, place the fish stock and cream in a saucepan and boil until reduced by about half. Lower the heat and whisk in the cream cheese until smooth, then stir in the chives. Season to taste with lemon juice, cayenne, salt and freshly ground pepper.

Cook the quails' eggs in boiling salted water for 1½-2 minutes for soft-boiled eggs; allow 3 minutes for hard-boiled eggs. Drain the eggs and plunge them immediately into cold water. Drain once more, then peel the eggs at once.

To assemble, top each potato cake with a strip of smoked salmon shaped in a round. Set 2 quails' eggs in the centre of each and spoon a little sauce over the tops. Serve at once.

PICATOSTES WITH FRUIT COMPOTE

This Spanish breakfast dish is popular at Easter and Christmas. Dry out the bread the day before you plan to serve it.

Serves 4-6

good-quality white bread or brioche
150ml/¼ pint milk, plus 1 tbsp extra
4 tsp caster sugar, plus extra for dusting
½ tsp ground cinnamon, plus extra for dusting
2 eggs, beaten
vegetable oil for deep frying

FRUIT COMPOTE
170g/6oz ready-to-eat dried apricots
115g/4oz ready-to-eat stoned prunes
55g/2oz sultanas
300ml/½ pint fresh orange juice
2 oranges and 2 bananas
natural yogurt, to serve

Cut the bread in 2cm/¾in-thick slices, then stamp out 16 small seasonal shapes, such as rabbits, ducks, chickens or lambs with biscuit cutters. Place in a single layer on a tray and leave for 24 hours to dry out. Alternatively, pre-heat the oven to its lowest setting and bake the bread for 10-15 minutes until it dries out, turning it once. Leave to cool.

To make the fruit compote, place the apricots, prunes and sultanas in a saucepan with the orange juice and 300ml/½ pint water. Bring to the boil. Remove the pan from the heat, cover and leave for at least 24 hours. (It will keep like this in the refrigerator for 3-4 days.)

Just before frying the *picatostes*, peel the oranges, removing all the white pith, and remove each segment from the central membrane with a small sharp knife. Peel and slice the bananas and then add the fresh fruit to the compote.

To fry the *picatostes*, heat the 150ml/¼ pint milk with the sugar and cinnamon, then dip each bread shape in the milk to moisten it. Heat the oil in a deep-fat fryer to 180C/360F, or until a cube of bread browns in about 40 seconds. Beat the eggs with 1 tbsp milk and dip each shape quickly. Deep fry in batches until golden brown. Drain the shapes well on kitchen paper. Sprinkle with sugar and ground cinnamon to taste. Serve the *picatostes* immediately with the compote and natural yogurt.

EASTER LUNCH

GAMMON COOKED IN SPICED CIDER WITH A SWEET MUSTARD CRUST
Serves 10

*2.3-2.5kg/5-5½lb piece smoked or green
gammon
12 whole black peppercorns
12 whole cloves
2 bay leaves
1 large onion, quartered
1 large carrot, cut in chunks
1 celery stick, cut in chunks
about 3 litres/5 pints dry cider
45g/1½oz fresh white breadcrumbs
85g/3oz demerara sugar
1½ tbsp Dijon mustard
2 tbsp cornflour*

POTATO NESTS FILLED WITH SPRING VEGETABLES
*1 medium cooking apple, about
225g/8oz
900g/2lb potatoes, peeled and
roughly chopped
salt
30g/1oz butter, plus extra for
greasing trays
1 egg yolk
10 button onions
10 baby carrots
20 fine asparagus tips
10 mangetout*

Place the gammon in a large saucepan in which it fits quite snugly. Add the peppercorns, cloves, bay leaves, onion, carrot and celery, and pour in enough cider to completely cover the gammon. Bring slowly to the boil, then lower the heat, cover and simmer for 30 minutes per 450g/1lb (2½-2¾ hours).

While the gammon is simmering, quarter, peel and core the apple. Cook it in the simmering liquid for about 20 minutes until just tender. Drain well and mash to make a simple apple purée. Set aside.

Meanwhile, prepare the potato nests. Steam the potatoes until tender for 20-30 minutes depending on their size. Transfer to a clean saucepan and mash with a potato masher. Cook over gentle heat, stirring all the time, until the potato is fairly dry. Remove from the heat and stir in salt to taste, then beat in the butter. Finally beat in the egg yolk and leave to cool. Butter two baking trays.

Using a piping bag fitted with a medium star nozzle (No. 8), pipe ten nests of potato on to the greased baking trays. To shape the nests, start in the centre and work outwards in a continuous movement. Pipe three concentric rings of potato on to the tray to form the base, then continue piping but this time pipe two contin-

LEFT CURED HAM IS A TRADITIONAL SPRING CELEBRATION DISH IN NORTHERN EUROPE AND AMERICA.

uous circles, one on top of the other, on the outside edge of each base to form the sides. Set aside.

Pre-heat the oven to 220C/ 425F/Gas 7. Remove the gammon from the cooking liquid and leave to cool a little. Reserve the cooking liquid. To make the crust for the gammon, combine the breadcrumbs, sugar and mustard.

Remove the strings from the gammon joint and peel away the skin. Score the fat with a small sharp knife, then press the breadcrumb mixture all over the surface of the fat. Set the gammon in a roasting tin and cover the cut face of the meat with buttered foil. Place the gammon in the oven with the potato nests and roast for about 30 minutes until the gammon crust and potato nests are golden brown.

Meanwhile, cook the vegetables in the reserved cooking liquid – the onions take about 25 minutes, carrots about 10 minutes and the asparagus and mangetout 2 minutes. Drain well and keep warm. If necessary, cut the vegetables so they will fit in the potato nests. Warm the apple purée.

Strain 600ml/1 pint of the cooking liquid into a small saucepan. Mix the cornflour with a little water and stir into the cooking liquid. Bring to the boil, then lower the heat and simmer, stirring, until thickened.

To serve, arrange the gammon on a large serving platter and surround with the potato nests. Fill each nest with a spoonful of apple purée and top with the vegetables. Serve the sauce separately.

ITALIAN EASTER PIE
La Torta Pasqualina

Traditionally, this Genoese pie should consist of 33 layers of pastry – one for each year of Christ's life – made with flour, oil and water (commercial filo pastry makes a good substitute), fresh young chard or spinach leaves, soft cheese and fresh eggs. If using chard, use a good amount of leaf and keep surplus stalks for use in another recipe (they are delicious blanched then tossed in butter).

This variation of the pie combines the chopped greens with the herbs and cheese, then the mixture is lightened in texture by adding milk-soaked breadcrumbs and beaten eggs. Some people like to layer the ingredients but this method gives a denser and more satisfactory filling.

Serves 8-12

1.5kg/3lb Swiss chard or spinach leaves
salt and freshly ground black pepper
15g/½oz fresh marjoram leaves
350g/12oz ricotta cheese, or cottage cheese
200g/7oz fresh Parmesan cheese, grated
9 eggs
125ml/4fl oz milk
55g/2oz fresh white breadcrumbs
400g/14oz filo pastry, thawed if frozen
85g/3oz unsalted butter, melted

Rinse the chard or spinach leaves. Remove the stalks and cut them into 5cm/2in lengths. Cook the stalks in boiling salted water for 3-5 minutes until just tender, then remove with a slotted spoon. Add the leaves to the same boiling water and bring back to the boil, then drain well. Squeeze the excess water from all the greens by wrapping them in a clean tea towel and twisting the ends in opposite directions. Leave to cool, then coarsely chop the stalks and leaves and transfer to a large bowl.

Add the marjoram, ricotta or cottage cheese, 170g/6oz of the Parmesan cheese, 3 eggs, milk and breadcrumbs to the greens. Season very generously with salt and pepper and beat thoroughly until evenly combined. (It is a good idea to cook a tiny amount of the mixture in a small frying pan, or in the microwave to check the seasoning.)

Pre-heat the oven to 200C/400F/ Gas 6.

Lay out the filo pastry on a sheet of cling film and keep one-third covered with extra cling film to prevent it drying. This portion will make the top of the pie.

Grease a 23cm/9in non-stick springform cake tin with a little of the melted butter. Lay a sheet of filo pastry in the tin, letting the pastry

RIGHT ITALIAN EASTER PIE MADE WITH FRESH CHARD, AND SMOKED LAMB SALAD.

edges fall over the sides. Brush the filo with butter. Continue layering up the pastry, buttering between each sheet and pressing the pastry into the sides of the tin. It does not matter how you do this – if the pastry breaks it can easily be patched.

Spoon the filling into the pastry case and level the surface. Make six large indentations in the surface using the back of a spoon. Crack the remaining eggs, one at a time, and carefully set one in each indentation without breaking the yolk. Season to taste and sprinkle with the remaining Parmesan cheese.

Fold in the overlapping pastry, then top with the remaining pastry in layers, brushing with butter between each layer. This can be done in a fairly haphazard way with folds to produce a decorative effect to the finished pie. Brush with the last of the butter, then with a little cold water. Bake the pie for 1½ hours until the pastry is crisp and golden.

Leave the pie to cool in the tin. *Torta Pasqualina* should be served just warm to bring out the best of the rich flavours.

SPRING SALAD WITH SMOKED WELSH LAMB

I first sampled smoked Welsh lamb at a country fair and found it so delicious and perfect for a spring salad. Other smoked meats, such as chicken or duck may be substituted, but I recommend you do try to find Welsh lamb. It is available from good delicatessens and through gourmet mail order suppliers (see page 126).
Serves 4

225g/8oz assorted salad leaves
10g/¼oz fresh flat-leaf parsley or chervil leaves
10g/¼oz fresh mint or coriander leaves
3 tbsp chopped chives
225g/8oz freshly cooked new potatoes, preferably Jersey, thickly sliced
115g/4oz small mangetout, blanched and sliced if large
Honey Mustard Dressing (see below)
salt and freshly ground black pepper
350g/12oz oak-smoked Welsh lamb or other smoked meat, thinly sliced
4 fresh mint sprigs

Rinse and pat dry the salad leaves, then tear them into bite-sized pieces.

Combine the salad leaves with the herbs, new potatoes and mangetout in a large bowl. Add dressing to taste and toss well until all the leaves are lightly coated and glistening. Season to taste.

Arrange the salad on four dinner plates. Set the slices of lamb on top and garnish with the mint sprigs. Serve at once.

HONEY MUSTARD DRESSING

This dressing keeps well in the refrigerator in a screw-topped jar for up to a week.
Makes about 350ml/12fl oz

250 ml/8fl oz vegetable oil
4 tbsp red wine vinegar
4 tbsp acacia honey
2 tbsp Dijon mustard
1 tbsp finely chopped onion
salt and freshly ground black pepper

Shake all the ingredients together in a screw-topped jar and season to taste.

ROAST CHICKEN WITH SPRING HERBS AND LEMON GRAVY
Serves 4

1.5kg/3½lb oven-ready free-range chicken
15g/½oz fresh tarragon
15g/½oz fresh parsley
15g/½oz fresh chives, chopped
1 lemon
85g/3oz unsalted butter, softened
salt and freshly ground black pepper
4 tbsp dry white wine
175ml/6fl oz chicken stock
1 tbsp cornflour
extra tarragon, flat-leaf parsley and chives, to garnish

Wipe the chicken inside and over the surface of the skin with a clean damp cloth. Pre-heat the oven to 190C/ 375F/Gas 5.

Remove the herb leaves from their stalks. Reserve the stalks and chop the leaves finely. Mix with the chopped chives and 1 tbsp of lemon juice squeezed from the lemon. Work in the softened butter and season.

Using your fingers, carefully loosen the skin of the chicken where it covers the breasts and legs, then press the herb butter under the skin over the breasts and legs.

Cut the lemon into large chunks and place these in the cavity of the chicken with the reserved herb stalks. Season the bird with salt and pepper, place in a roasting tin and pour 150ml/¼ pint water around the bird. Roast the chicken for 1½-1¾ hours, basting occasionally, until golden and tender when tested with a skewer through the thickest part of the thigh. The juices should be clear.

Transfer the chicken to a serving platter and leave to rest in a warm place. Place the roasting tin over the heat and bring the cooking juices to the boil. Pour in the white wine and simmer gently. Stir the chicken stock into the cornflour until smooth, then pour into the pan. Cook, stirring, until thickened, then season to taste. Pass the gravy through a fine sieve into a warmed sauceboat.

Garnish the roast chicken with small bouquets of fresh herbs and serve with the sauce.

LEMON SNAP BASKETS
Makes 8

BISCUIT BASKETS
55g/2oz butter
55g/2oz caster sugar
85g/3oz golden syrup
1 tsp lemon juice

55g/2oz plain flour
1 tsp finely grated lemon zest

LEMON MOUSSE
115g/4oz caster sugar
finely grated rind of 1 large lemon
juice of 2 large lemons
4 eggs, separated
1 tbsp powdered gelatine
150ml/¼ pint double cream

DECORATION
whipped cream
pansies, primroses or other spring
flowers, or fresh fruit

To make the biscuit baskets, pre-heat the oven to 180C/350F/Gas 4. Line one or two baking trays with baking parchment, or use non-stick trays.

Place the butter, sugar and syrup in a small saucepan and heat gently, stirring, until the butter melts. Remove from the heat and stir in the remaining ingredients. Leave to cool.

LEFT LEMON SNAP BASKETS FULL OF THE FRESHNESS OF SPRING

Divide the mixture into eight portions and spoon two portions well apart on to a baking tray. Cook in batches for 10-12 minutes until each biscuit is flattened and golden. Allow to cool slightly on the tray, then remove and place each one over a small ramekin dish and shape it into a basket. Leave to cool and harden. Repeat the process until you have eight baskets. Store in an air-tight container until required.

To make the lemon mousse, dissolve the sugar in 150ml/¼ pint water in a small saucepan over a gentle heat. Add the lemon rind and juice and simmer for 6 minutes.

Place the egg yolks in a bowl and whisk with a hand-held electric whisk for 1 minute, then pour on the lemon syrup, whisking continuously. Dissolve the gelatine in 4 tbsp of water in a small saucepan over very gentle heat, then whisk this into the egg mixture. Chill the mousse for about 1 hour until beginning to set.

Whisk the egg whites until stiff and whip the cream to the 'floppy' stage. Fold the cream into the lemon mousse, then fold in the egg whites. Cover and chill for at least 3 hours until set.

To serve, fill each basket with two scoops of lemon mousse. Top with a whirl of whipped cream, then decorate with flowers or fruit.

MAD HATTER'S TEA PARTY

SANDWICH PLATTER
Makes 64 triangles

20 slices brown bread
150g/5oz butter, softened
300g/10oz cucumber, thinly sliced
12 slices white bread
crisp green salad leaves, such as
watercress, rocket, mustard and cress
or lettuce

SALMON FILLING
418g/14¾oz can red salmon
1 tbsp powdered gelatine
250ml/8fl oz mayonnaise or
double cream
1 tbsp lemon juice
1 tbsp tomato ketchup
ground white pepper

EGG AND ANCHOVY FILLING
8 canned anchovy fillets, well drained
4 tbsp mayonnaise
6 hard-boiled eggs, shelled
ground white pepper

To make the salmon filling, drain and reserve the juice from the salmon but discard the skin and bones. Dissolve the gelatine in 3 tbsp cold water in a small saucepan over very gentle heat.

Place the mayonnaise or cream, lemon juice and tomato ketchup in a food processor and whizz in the gelatine. Add the salmon with its liquid and pulse quickly to combine but keep a slightly rough texture. Season to taste with pepper.

Transfer to a dish, cover with cling film and chill for at least 3 hours until firmly set. (This can be made up to 48 hours in advance and kept, covered, in the refrigerator.)

To make the egg and anchovy filling, mash the anchovies to a paste on a plate or board with the back of a round-ended knife. Combine well with the mayonnaise. Mash the eggs and stir into the anchovy-flavoured mayonnaise. Season generously with white pepper.

To make the sandwiches, spread a generous amount of salmon filling on to 10 slices of lightly buttered brown bread and top with thinly sliced cucumber. Season to taste. Top each with a second slice of lightly buttered bread and remove the crusts. Cut the sandwiches into 40 triangles.

Spread a generous amount of anchovy filling on to 6 slices of lightly buttered white bread and top with crisp green salad leaves. Top each with a second slice of lightly buttered bread. Remove the crusts and cut into 24 triangles. Cover with cling film if not serving at once.

RIGHT A DELICIOUS TEATIME SPREAD OF DAINTY SANDWICHES, EASTER BONNET BISCUITS AND CHOCOLATE GATEAU.

EASTER BONNET BISCUITS
Makes about 12

115g/4oz plain flour
75g/2½oz caster sugar
55g/2oz ground almonds
pinch of salt
100g/3½oz unsalted butter, plus extra
for greasing
1 egg yolk
400g/14oz ready-to-roll icing
edible food colourings
3 tbsp apricot jam, warmed and sieved
about 12 marshmallows or other soft
round jelly sweets
icing sugar
about 4 tbsp Royal Icing (page 17)

Place the flour, sugar, ground almonds, salt and butter in a food processor and pulse quickly until the mixture is the consistency of fine crumbs. Add the egg yolk and pulse to make a soft dough. Turn out the

LEFT EASTER BONNET BISCUITS CONTAIN A SURPRISE MARSHMALLOW.

dough and knead lightly with floured hands to give a smooth shape, then wrap in cling film and chill for at least 1 hour. Meanwhile, grease a baking tray.

Roll out half the dough on a lightly floured surface until 3mm/⅛in thick (keep the other half in the refrigerator). Stamp out fluted rounds with an 8cm/3¼in biscuit cutter. Re-roll the trimmings with the remaining chilled dough to make about 12 biscuits. Set the biscuits on the baking tray. Chill for a further 20 minutes. Meanwhile, pre-heat the oven to 190C/375F/Gas 5. Bake the biscuits for 10-12 minutes until golden brown. Transfer to a wire rack and leave to cool completely.

Knead 350g/12oz of the icing with a few drops of colouring to give a soft pastel colour. Divide the remaining icing and colour each portion with a different colour, then wrap all the icings in cling film.

Brush each biscuit with warm apricot jam, then set a marshmallow or sweet in the centre of each one .

Roll out the large portion of icing on a surface lightly sprinkled with icing sugar. Stamp out fluted rounds with a 9.5cm/3¾in biscuit cutter. Press one icing round over the top of each biscuit to form the bonnet.

Use the trimmings and other coloured icings to make tiny flowers, using a small flower cutter. Attach these to each bonnet with a little royal icing. Pipe a dot of icing in the centre of each flower and leave to set. Store in an air-tight container.

CHOCOLATE GATEAU
Makes 12 slices

FOR THE SPONGE
115g/4oz plain flour
4 tbsp cocoa powder
4 eggs
150g/5oz caster sugar
3 tbsp melted butter, plus extra for
greasing

FOR THE SYRUP
100g/3½oz caster sugar
4 tbsp Cointreau or other orange-
flavoured liqueur

FOR THE FILLING
250ml/8fl oz double cream
200g/7oz plain chocolate, broken
into pieces
5 tbsp cocoa powder, sifted
120g/4½oz unsalted butter, softened
2 tbsp icing sugar, sifted
2 tbsp Cointreau or other orange-
flavoured liqueur

FOR THE DECORATION
12 chocolate egg runouts (pages 12-13)

Butter and line the base of a 23cm/9in cake tin with greaseproof paper or baking parchment. Pre-heat the oven to 200C/400F/Gas 6.

Sift together the flour and cocoa powder. Whisk the eggs and sugar in a bowl set over a saucepan of simmering water with a hand-held electric whisk until the mixture is mousse-like and thick enough to leave a trail when the beaters are lifted. Remove from the heat. Fold in the flour and cocoa in batches, then fold in the melted butter.

Transfer the mixture to the prepared tin and bake for about 20 minutes until risen and just firm to the touch – the cake should spring back when pressed. Allow to cool slightly in the tin, then turn out on to a wire rack to cool completely.

To make the syrup, dissolve the sugar in 175ml/6fl oz water in a small saucepan over gentle heat. Bring to the boil, then remove from the heat. Allow to cool, then stir in the liqueur and set aside to cool.

To make the filling, heat the cream and chocolate in a saucepan over medium heat until the chocolate melts, then stir until thoroughly mixed. Remove from the heat. Beat the cocoa powder, butter and icing sugar together until light and fluffy, then beat in the cold chocolate cream a little at a time. Beat in the liqueur .

Slice the cake horizontally into three layers. Moisten the bottom layer thoroughly with a generous third of the syrup. Use about one quarter of the filling to sandwich the layers back together, moistening each layer with a third of the syrup just before layering, then use about half the remaining filling to cover the sides and top of the cake. Place the rest of the filling in a piping bag fitted with a medium star nozzle (No. 8) and pipe 12 whirls around the outside edge of the cake.

Set a little Easter egg on each whirl. Store in a cool place.

TRADITIONAL EASTER CAKES

MAZUREK KROLEWSKI

This Polish cake is a traditional Easter sweetmeat. There are many different recipes, but this one combines a rich almond pastry base with a wonderful morello cherry jam topping. Other variations include spreading the pastry base with a thin layer of plum jam and then topping it with almond paste and chocolate, or decorating with a thin layer of meringue, candied peel and nuts.

Makes about 16 slices

225g/8oz self-raising flour
55g/2oz butter, softened, plus extra for greasing
55g/2oz ground almonds
55g/2oz caster sugar
1 whole egg plus 1 egg yolk
1½ tbsp natural yogurt or soured cream
¼ tsp arak flavouring (optional)
¼ tsp natural vanilla essence
lightly beaten egg white, to glaze
morello cherry jam, preferably Polish

Pre-heat the oven to 180C/350F/Gas 4 and lightly grease a baking tray.

Sift the flour into a bowl, then rub in the butter. Stir in the ground almonds and sugar.

Beat the egg, egg yolk and yogurt or soured cream together with the arak flavouring, if using, and vanilla essence and add to the dry ingredients. Mix well to make a firm dough.

Roll out about two-thirds of the dough on a lightly floured surface into a 19cm/7½in square and trim the edges. Transfer to the prepared baking tray and prick with a fork, then brush with beaten egg white.

Combine the reserved dough and the trimmings and roll out about 5mm/¼in thick. Cut several lengths of dough about 1.5cm/½in wide, then cut and fit to make a border around the edges of the square of dough. Arrange the rest in diagonal lines, cutting as necessary to make an abstract arrangement. Mark with a fork or small cutter to give a decorative effect. Brush with egg white.

Bake the cake for 20-25 minutes until golden brown. Carefully transfer to a wire rack.

Spoon a generous quantity of jam into the spaces on the top of the *mazurek* and spread it neatly to the corners. Leave to cool completely.

117

COLOMBA

Colomba is the Italian word for dove, and this sweet yeast cake from Lombardy is traditionally cooked in the shape of the bird. Recipes vary as to whether it should have sultanas or candied fruit inside – here candied orange peel and chopped almonds have also been added – but there is no controversy about the topping which is always sugar crystals and whole blanched almonds. Traditionally, the Italians are more likely to buy this in their local *pasticceria* than make it, hence the tremendous choice of beautifully boxed *colomba* available in delicatessens during the Easter season.

Makes 16 slices

ABOVE TRADITIONAL EASTER CAKES –
COLOMBA, MAZUREK KROLEWSKI AND
SIMNEL CAKE DECORATED WITH MARZIPAN
DAFFODILS TO REPRESENT THE APOSTLES.

30g/1oz fresh yeast, or 15g/½oz dried yeast
150ml/¼ pint milk, lukewarm
400g/14oz strong white flour
3 egg yolks
55g/2oz caster sugar
1 tsp salt
finely grated rind of ½ lemon
pinch grated nutmeg
115g/4oz unsalted butter, softened, plus extra for greasing
115g/4oz candied orange peel, chopped
55g/2oz blanched almonds, chopped
lightly beaten egg white or melted

butter, to glaze
55g/2oz white sugar cubes, roughly crushed
30g/1oz whole blanched almonds

Crumble the fresh yeast into a bowl and cream it to a smooth liquid with the milk. Stir in 2 tbsp of the flour, then cover and leave the mixture for about 20 minutes to become frothy. If using dried yeast, mix the granules with the milk and 1 tsp of the sugar and set aside, covered, for about 15 minutes until frothy.

Place the egg yolks, sugar, salt and lemon rind in a large bowl and beat well. Stir in the yeast mixture. Beat in half the remaining flour with the nutmeg, then gradually beat in the softened butter. Add the remaining flour and mix to form a soft dough.

Turn out the dough on to a lightly floured surface and knead for about 10 minutes until light and springy. Shape the dough into a ball, place it inside a greased polythene bag and tie the bag closed. Leave the dough to rise for about 1 hour until doubled in size. Meanwhile, grease a 22cm/8¾in springform cake tin.

Turn out the risen dough on to a lightly floured surface. Knock back and knead in the chopped orange peel and almonds. Shape the dough into a ball and place in the prepared tin, pushing down well with your knuckles so it fills the base of the tin. Brush with beaten egg white or melted butter and sprinkle with the sugar and almonds. Cover with a clean tea towel and leave to rise in a warm place for about 40 minutes, or until the dough just reaches the top of the tin. Meanwhile, pre-heat the oven to 200C/400F/Gas 6.

Bake the loaf for 20 minutes, then reduce the heat to 180C/350F/Gas 4 and bake for a further 20-25 minutes until the bread sounds hollow when unmoulded and tapped on the bottom.

Transfer to a wire rack and leave to cool completely.

Serve in slices, spread with butter, if wished.

SIMNEL CAKE

Simnel cake was originally made for Mothering Sunday in Britain but has now become more usually known as an Easter cake. Tradition has it that the marzipan should be stamped with the figure of Christ and surrounded by small marzipan balls representing the apostles. There is argument as to the number – 11 or 12 – depending on whether Judas is included.

Makes 16-20 slices

200g/7oz plain flour
pinch of salt
2 tsp ground mixed spice
170g/6oz butter, softened, plus extra for greasing
170g/6oz light muscovado sugar
finely grated rind of 1 orange
4 eggs, beaten

170g/6oz currants
170g/6oz sultanas
170g/6oz raisins
85g/3oz glacé cherries
55g/2oz cut mixed peel
350g/12oz Marzipan (page 15)
icing sugar for rolling

DECORATION
400g/14oz Marzipan (page 15)
edible food colouring
1 egg white, lightly beaten
3 tbsp apricot jam, warmed and sieved
1 tbsp Royal Icing (page 16), optional

Preheat the oven to 160C/325F/Gas 3. Grease a 20cm/8in round cake tin with butter and line with a double thickness of greaseproof paper. Tie a thick band of brown paper around the outside of the tin and stand it on a pad of paper on a baking tray.

Sift the flour, salt and spice together. Cream the butter and sugar together with the orange rind until pale and fluffy. Beat in the eggs, a little at a time, adding a little flour if the egg starts to curdle (this often happens when using brown sugar). Fold in the remaining flour and fruit. Place half the cake mixture in the prepared tin and level the surface.

Roll out the marzipan on a surface lightly sprinkled with icing sugar into a 20cm/8in circle. Lay the marzipan circle on top of the cake mixture and press down lightly. Spoon the remaining cake mixture on top and level the surface.

Bake the cake for about 2½ hours until risen and golden and a skewer inserted into the centre comes out hot and clean. Do not confuse the marzipan with raw cake mixture when doing this test. Leave the cake to cool in the tin.

To decorate, colour 115g/4oz of the marzipan with green food colouring. Colour the rest with yellow food colouring. Roll out a generous half of the yellow marzipan on a surface lightly sprinkled with icing sugar. Cut 12 strips, each 2cm/¾in wide and 5cm/2in long. Make small cuts along the long edge of each strip, then roll up to make the centre of a daffodil. Using a small oval cutter, stamp out 72 petal shapes. Attach six of these 'petals' to each daffodil trumpet, using a little egg white if necessary. Set aside.

Collect all the trimmings and add to the rest of the yellow marzipan. Re-roll into a 20cm/8in circle and attach to the top of the cake using a little apricot glaze.

Divide the green marzipan into four equal pieces and roll each one into a fine rope about 40cm/16in long. Taking two ropes at a time, twist them round each other to make a rope effect. Attach these ropes round the outside edge of the cake using a little apricot glaze and cutting to fit as necessary. Arrange the daffodils on top of the cake, and if wished, pipe an Easter message on top of the cake in royal icing.

ORIGAMI DUCK
pp.72-3

1 Fold a square of paper in half diagonally and crease. Unfold, then fold lower edges to centre line.

2 Fold upper edges to centre crease.

3 Fold in half along centre line (mountain fold).

4&5 Fold bottom point up inside model (inside reverse fold)

6 Fold right-hand point down (inside reverse fold)

7 Fold bottom point up (inside reverse fold)

8 Outside reverse fold to form head. Crease along dotted lines.

9 Make beak by folding in on itself along creases (double reverse fold)

10 Fold up bottom point into duck. Turn over and repeat on other side.

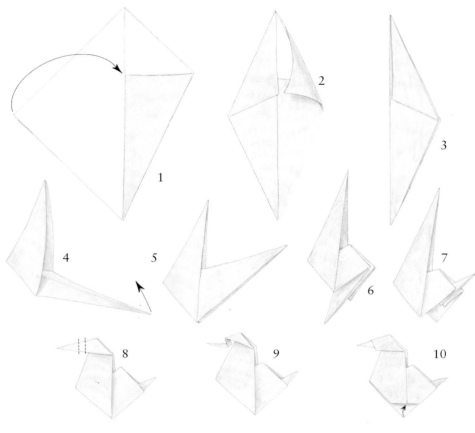

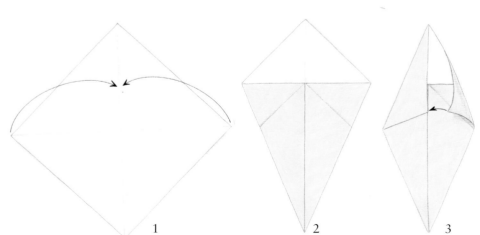

ORIGAMI CHICK
pp.72-3

1&2 Fold a square of paper in half diagonally. Crease. Unfold, then fold lower edges to centre.

3 Fold in upper edges to centre line.

4 Fold in half horizontally.

5 Unfold steps 3 and 4. Lift inner right-hand corner and bring down towards bottom point. Flatten.

6 Repeat with inner left-hand corner to make new diamond shape. Turn so small wings point to the right.

7 Fold in half so the open edges are on the top. Crease along the dotted line.

8 Bring left hand point upwards around the form. The model will open up slightly during this fold.

9 Flatten folds and crease.

10 Fold upper point to the left opening it around the model.

11 Flatten folds and crease.

12 Form beak by folding in on itself (double reverse fold).

13 Fold wing forward along dotted line.

14 Crease in forward position.

15 Fold wing back on itself so the point extends above the chick's back. Crease. Repeat steps 13-15 on the other side.

16 Fold tail in on itself (inside reverse fold).

17 Fold bottom point back up inside and flatten out to the side.

18 Fold right-hand point back in on itself again to form foot (inside reverse fold).

19 Turn back lower corners in to finish off.

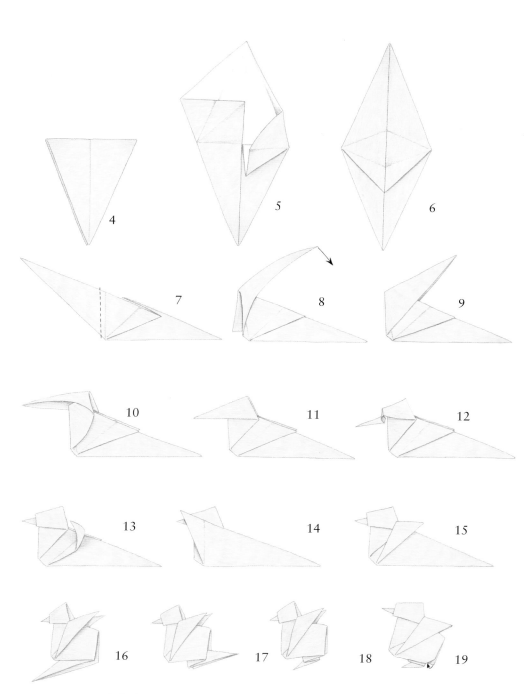

EASTER MOTIFS

Whether you want to make cards, bake biscuits, appliqué clothes, or simply decorate plain tissue paper for wrappings, the addition of an Easter motif makes them immediately seasonal. Either trace these shapes straight off the page, or size them up or down on a photocopying machine to achieve the proportions you need.

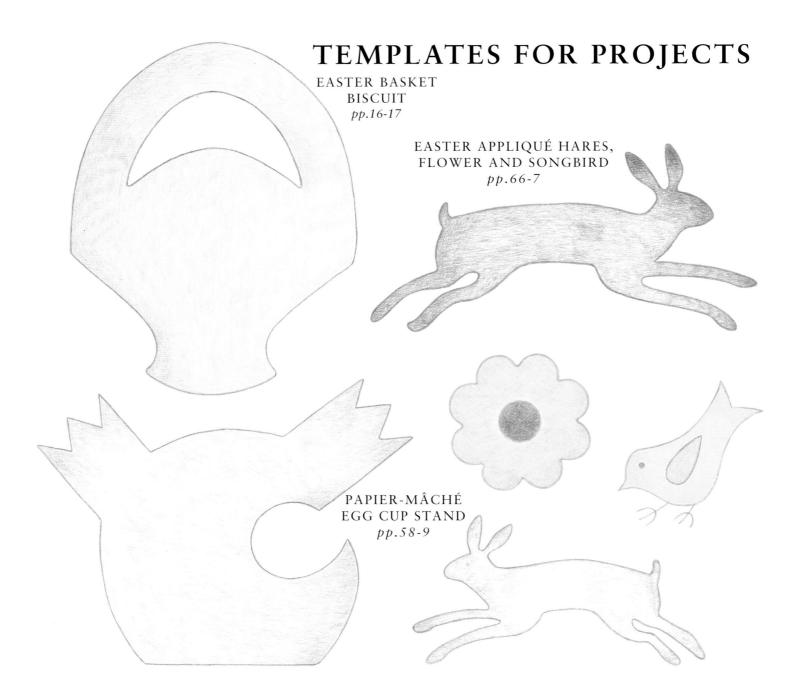

TEMPLATES FOR PROJECTS

EASTER BASKET
BISCUIT
pp.16-17

EASTER APPLIQUÉ HARES,
FLOWER AND SONGBIRD
pp.66-7

PAPIER-MÂCHÉ
EGG CUP STAND
pp.58-9

EASTER BONNET DECORATIONS
pp.68-71

SQUARE CONCERTINA

Cut two strips of coloured paper and fix them together at right angles with double-sided sticky tape. Fold A over B, then B over A. Repeat until you reach the ends and secure these with double-sided tape.

Either use the concertina as it is or make it into a full or half rosette . Half rosettes are required to trim the Top Hat and full rosettes to trim the Poke Bonnet.

SPIRAL CONCERTINA

Cut two strips of coloured paper and trim their ends to an angle of 45°. Do this by folding back the corner of a squared-off end until the top edge of the strip aligns exactly with the side. Carefully cut along the crease. By cutting the ends to this angle, the concertina will automatically fold into a long spiral strip. Fix the ends, and fold the strips as for the square concertina, being careful to preserve the 45° angle down the full length of the spiral, otherwise it will gradually straighten itself out.

ACKNOWLEDGMENTS

CONTRIBUTORS

Karin Cafazzo-Hossack (batik eggs pp.28-31, springtime sweater pp.60-5)
32 Petley Road, London W6 9ST
(071 386 9748)

Carluccio's (pasta nests pp. 44-5)
30 Neal Street, London WC2H 9PS
(071 240 1487)

Shane Connolly (fresh flowers pp.76-89)
7 Bracewell Road, London W10 6AE
(081 964 4398)

Georgina Crowder (gilded eggs pp. 32-3)
(081 673 3641) or at Abbey Frames
(071 622 4815)

Jamboree (appliqué children's clothes pp.66-7)
c/o Barnshill Cottage, Thornden Lane,
Rolvenden Layne, Rolvenden,
Nr Cranbrook, Kent

Alison Jenkins (Easter bonnets pp.68-71)
36 Crystal Palace Road, London SE22 9HB

Susan Moxley (papier-mâché gift boxes pp. 46-9)
33 Edith Road, Grandpont,
Oxford OX1 4QB (0865 251396)

Jane Packer (topiary eggs pp. 94-7)
56 James Street, London W1M 5HS
(071 935 2673)

Juliette Pearce (papier-mâché egg cup pp.58-9)
Cross Street Studios, 14 Cross Street,
Hove BN3 1AJ (0273 725321)

Martin Robinson (egg and feather wreath pp.50-1, spring urns pp.74-5,
moss hare pp.90-1)
Martin Robinson Flowers, Thomas Neal's,
Earlham Street, London WC2H 9LD
(071 379 3201)

Royal School of Needlework (cross-stitch sampler pp.52-3)
Apartment 12a, Hampton Court Palace, East Molesey, Surrey KT8 9AU (081 943 1432)

Deborah Schneebeli-Morrell (natural dyed eggs pp. 24-5, engraved eggs pp. 26-7, papercut cards pp.54-7)
10 York Rise, London NW5 1SS

Mark at Juliet Willis (dried flower nest pp. 92-3)
336 Old York Road, London SW18 1SS
(081 874 9944)

Basia Zarzycka (beaded eggs pp. 34-7)
135 King's Road, London SW3 4PW
(071 351 7276)

SUPPLIERS

ARTIST'S AND GILDING MATERIALS
L. Cornelissen & Son Ltd, 105 Russell Street, London WC1 (071 636 1045)

Stuart Stevenson, 68 Clerkenwell Road, London EC1M 5QA (071 253 1693)

BATIK EQUIPMENT
Dryad Craft Centre, 178 Kensington High Street, London W8 (071 937 5370). Mail order available.

CRAFT PAPERS AND EGG-DYING KITS
Paperchase, 213 Tottenham Court Road, London W1P 9AF (071 580 8496). Mail order available.

NATURAL DYE MATERIALS
Jenny Dean, Ashill Studio, Boundary Cottage, 172 Clifton Road, Shefford, Bedfordshire SG17 5AH (0462 812001)

SPECIALITY MEATS
Fjordling Smokehouses, Dunstable Farm, Pitton Road, West Winterslow, Salisbury, Wiltshire SP5 1SA (0980 862 689)

The publishers would like to thank the following for their help with props:

Appalachia, 14a George Street, St Albans, Herts AL3 4ER
Ann Lingard, Rope Walk Antiques, Rye, Sussex TN31 7NA
Michael Snell (chocolatier), Michael Snell Tearooms, 8 St Thomas's Square, Salisbury, Wiltshire (0722 336037)
Juliet Willis, 336 Old York Road, London SW18 1SS

The author would also like to thank Jane Suthering for her luscious recipes, Shane Connolly for his delightful fresh flowers, Panadam Polish Delicatessen, 2 Marius Road, London SW17 7QQ for all their assistance and especially the whole team: Debbie Patterson for her evocative, painterly photographs; Mary Evans for her inspired creative direction; Prue Bucknall for her beautiful design and Jo Mead for so skilfully bringing the whole book together.

INDEX